Other Bool

Novels

Leverage

Incentivize

Deliverables

Heir Apparent (2013)

Non-Fiction

Lessons Learned the Hard Way (2013)

Navigating Corporate Politics

By Tom Spears

http://outofcorporatelife.blogspot.com/
http://www.tomspears.com/

Navigating Corporate Politics

Copyright © 2012 Tom Spears

For information contact the author at tspears62@gmail.com

DEDICATION

To Marion A. "Bud" Keyes, my mentor and the man who taught me more about surviving in the large corporations than everyone else combined.

ACKNOWLEDGMENTS

Soon after I retired in 2010, I began to blog. As time went on, I noticed that much of the material I was covering was related to the cryptic and poorly understood world of corporate politics.

Later, when I began to write corporate thrillers, I realized I needed to develop a credible, written basis for my expertise on corporations and the way they operate. I started with a white paper on corporate politics, and I later expanded this into a regular feature further developing on the basic ideas. Over time, the white paper and blog entries have become quite popular, and in effect, the idea for this book was born.

So you may be wondering what makes me an expert in corporate politics.

The answer: I started off with a solid grounding in organizational behavior as a student of John Kotter during my MBA studies at Harvard. Then I spent many years in upper management within three large U.S.-based corporations – three highly political corporations. I learned the hard way how to survive, and even thrive, surrounded by some amazingly adept political animals. I observed political experts – ones I labeled "maneuverers" and "street fighters" in the book – as they jockeyed for position, and readily sacrificed each other in an endless contest of one-upmanship. I also observed many others who were less adept – or less willing to engage in some of the darker elements of corporate politics – crash and burn. Some of the most egregious examples of these behaviors appear in the later chapters of this book.

I'm sure many of these expert politicians would not appreciate me identifying them here, and I'll oblige them. Ladies and gentlemen, you undoubtedly know who you are. I offer each of you my thanks for the education – one sometimes painful to receive. And additional thanks go to the many off-the-wall people I've met during my career – you've provided a wealth of material, and the inspiration to write all of this down.

Heather Tahtinen, your reading and editing aid helped me make sure this material would be properly targeted and understood by my desired audience.

This book would resemble a collection of poorly integrated one-off blog posts if it wasn't for the help of my two proofreading friends. Mike Miller and Paula Kort – thank you for your help and assistance.

I owe a debt of gratitude to my family, particularly to those who stood next to me as I experienced those sometimes unbearable corporate years. Paula, Kenneth, Emily, and Anna – thank you for your tolerance and patience with all the missed events and my long trips and many hours spent away.

And a special thanks to "Bud" Keyes, a man I considered my mentor, and the person who first helped me understand the politics of large organizations and how to survive them.

Preface

This book is for new managers, who are just starting to figure out there is more to succeeding in corporations than what they teach you in an MBA program. It is also for professionals and mid-level managers who are trying to make sense of some of the crazy and seemingly pointless in-fighting they see going on in their organizations.

It is not targeted at senior executives, many of whom may bristle at some of the characterizations I use here to describe their behaviors. To them, I can only say – "I call 'em as I see 'em."

Now for a small confession: I've read a lot of business books over the years, and I've hated most of them.

Most of the authors offered only one or two new ideas, but demanded three hundred pages of reading in exchange for their wisdom. These "new" ideas were typically presented in the first couple of chapters with enough detail for the reader to grasp the high points. But normally it wasn't readily apparent that all the nuggets had been uncovered, requiring the reader to plow through page after page of filler, regurgitation, and repetitive example. I won't single out any particular book or author, but I'm sure if you're a student of business writing, you've observed this phenomena.

When I set out to write this book, I wanted to do something different. Many people have read my blog on corporate politics, and by listening to their feedback, I've tried to structure the book in a fashion that is more reader-friendly.

First, you will notice this book contains only 120 pages of text. I've tried to leave out all of the filler, drop most of the regurgitation, and sparingly use examples.

The first chapter gives you the big picture – corporate politics is pervasive, unavoidable, and necessary in large organizations. Pretending you can avoid or ignore it is done at great risk. By recognizing the situation, learning the company's politics, and engaging to the level you feel comfortable, you are helping yourself and those with whom you work. That might be enough for many readers. You'll get a whole book's worth of ideas in one chapter – and only need to read on if you want examples and additional detail. No sifting through two hundred pages looking for a few flakes of gold.

The next five chapters delve into details of the organizational context for your particular political environment – how your employers' history, size, leadership, and other factors will influence the degree of political harshness you may encounter.

Next you will find a series of chapters giving specific pointers on the techniques and tactics used within political environments. They are roughly arranged from most basic and safest to the most complex and risky. The reader need not visit any of these chapters unless they have interest in that specific technique.

I end with a recap and a few thoughts about where corporate political animals should go from here.

And that's it – shorter, quicker to the point, and hopefully without all the fluff.

July 20, 2012
Tom Spears

Table of Contents

Section 1 The Concept...**13**

   Chapter 1 – Navigating the Minefield...................................14

Section 2 The Corporate Environment **38**

   Chapter 2 – How Large is Large? 39

   Chapter 3 – How does History Impact Politics?................42

   Chapter 4 – How do Formal and Informal Rules Relate? .45

   Chapter 5 – The Style of the Top Dog Matters 48

   Chapter 6 – Power Players Beget more Power Players 52

   Chapter 7 – Politics and Position on the Ladder 54

   Chapter 8 – Avoiders..56

   Chapter 9 – Neutrals..58

   Chapter 10 – Power Players..62

Section 3 Tactics for Neutrals **66**

   Chapter 11 – Learn the Landscape..67

   Chapter 12 – Don't Burn Bridges...70

   Chapter 13 – Figure Out What's Valued 73

   Chapter 14 – Be Careful What you Put in Writing.............76

   Chapter 15 – Lend Support Before you Need it.................79

   Chapter 16 – Make Sure Risks are Tilted in your Favor 82

   Chapter 17 – Presentations Count...86

Chapter 18 – Don't Hide Bad News 89

Chapter 19 – Don't Badmouth Your Enemies 92

Chapter 20 – Keep Complaints to Yourself 95

Section 4 Tactics for Power Players 97

Chapter 21 – Actively Manage Your Reputation 98

Chapter 22 – Cultivate a Mentor 101

Chapter 23 – Ask for What You Want 105

Chapter 24 – Set the Bar Credibly Low 109

Chapter 25 – Provide Some Original Thinking 113

Chapter 26 – Promote Yourself 116

Chapter 27 – Distance Yourself from Failure 119

Chapter 28 – Expect Betrayal 122

Chapter 29 – Invest in Scapegoats 125

Chapter 30 – Use Sparingly, Use Strategically 129

Section 5 Final Thoughts 132

Chapter 31 – A Postscript 133

Section 1 – The Concept

Chapter 1 – Navigating the Minefield

Definitions:

Formal Corporate Rules – the official delegation of authority within an organization, usually described in written rules and limitations.

Informal Corporate Rules – the unofficial methods and channels within an organization that describe how things get done. Often these are extensions of formal corporate rules.

Corporate Rules – the integrated system of rules, methods and limitations included in both Formal and Informal Power systems.

Corporate Politics – the manipulation of Corporate Rules (formal and informal) to further a personal agenda.

Introduction:

Corporate politics and its impacts, have widespread negative connotations, yet the presence of politics is ubiquitous in large organizations. Corporate rules (formal and informal), on the other hand, at least appear to be grudgingly acknowledged as necessary, even if they are sometimes seen as a bit…unsavory. Both rules and politics are necessary for the normal functioning of large entities, and while proving this thesis is beyond the scope of this work, I offer as evidence the fact that incentive systems are implemented specifically to try to align personal agendas with the company's larger goals.

In this chapter, I use the metaphor of a "battlefield in a war-torn land" to describe the practical functions of both rules and politics. Rules are represented by the unexploded munitions obviously lying about, as well as by hidden mines. Political basics detail the skills employees should have to identify the bombs and mines and avoid tripping them. These techniques are described in greater detail in subsequent chapters. Beyond the basics are tools employees can use to deploy a few mines of their own – call them "advanced politics." Fail to learn the lessons and your career may be blown up. Master them and you may safely traverse the field to ascend higher up the corporate ladder.

A personal aside:

In my own climb up the ladder, I started off naïvely thinking performance was all that mattered – that hard work and superior achievement would ultimately lead to success. Of course, there is an element of truth to this belief – you won't succeed without the application of skill through hard work.

But it takes more.

It takes understanding how the organization makes judgments and decisions and the careful application of political capital to allow you to rise above the crowd.

Corporate ranks are filled with those who slave away for years but never get ahead.

One of my early performance reviews was summarized as "gets things done, but sometimes pisses people off." It took this deliberate wake-up call to get me to understand that there was more to winning the game than just notching big wins on projects.

Later, when I attended graduate school to receive my MBA, I became fascinated by the work of John Kotter on organizational structure, rules governing behavior, and power. While I wasn't yet keenly aware of my own behavior and how it might be seen by others, I was starting to understand what, other than just performance, was required to climb the corporate ladder.

I started to be able to read the political environment while I was working at Emerson Electric. It was there that a seasoned senior executive, Marion A. "Bud" Keyes, took me under his wing and explained what I was seeing. I learned more about business in my few years working for Bud than I did during the rest of my career.

By the time I was working for Valmont Industries, I was fully aware of corporate politics, knew instinctively what was at stake, and could sort through some of the commonly used "tricks of the trade." It was there that I was able to observe a series of master politicians interacting over a fairly long period of time. That showed me what worked and what didn't. It also illustrated the consequences and risks associated with all the different techniques I'll describe later in this book.

With the benefit of that hard earned wisdom, I can safely say you will never sustain yourself in a senior management position without understanding the workings of corporate politics.

Realities of formal and informal rules:

Large corporations – and by "large," I mean large enough that the Chief Executive cannot practically know all employees and their performance characteristics reasonably – employ both formal and informal power systems to manage and control the behaviors of employees. And the presence of these systems – plus the lack of direct understanding of what is happening by the boss – gives rise to politics within the organization.

Formal rules can most easily be seen in the form of written policies (and absence of them) and delegation of authority (or lack if it). These written, rules-based, behavior-limiting policies are the critical elements of the corporation's formal governance system.

Informal rule systems represent another set of policies and limitations. The primary difference between formal and informal rules is the ambiguity of the latter. Formal rules are generally fairly unambiguous, while informal rules are more open to (mis)interpretation.

The formal and informal rules that are present in the organization establish a series of norms and expected behaviors that employees must understand and are expected to follow. Both are often despised and disparaged by the employees that are controlled by them. You might hear someone rail about how the performance appraisal system is "unfair," or perhaps hear someone say: "But nobody said we couldn't look at porn on our laptops."

Politics are the intentional manipulation of perceptions to make one seem guilty, less guilty, or innocent of violations of the formal or informal rules. In politics, the "one" might be the person playing the games or someone else (often an unwitting victim).

Another environment where these systems operate is in a family with small children. The formal rules, while not necessarily written down, are usually pretty clear. For example, a "formal rule" might be the forbidding of lying. An "informal rule" would be an extension which says lying by omission is still lying. That might never have been specifically discussed, but should be readily understood by the children as a part of the basic formal (no lying) mandate. Yes, politics is also sometimes played in the family, but usually not normally with the skill found in corporations.

The difference between power and politics:
Corporate power is the ability to take action to change the course of the organization, or at least a small part of it. When we think of power, we usually think of organizational structure as granting that power, either through job title and responsibilities, reporting relationships, or formal and informal rules. These are the most obvious sources of power, but certainly not the only ones.

Some employees might be considered dangerous (or powerful) in an organization not because of any of the above, but simply because they have the CEO's ear. When I worked for one of my employers, I learned the hard way that one of my customer service managers was powerful because she had the ear of the big boss, and she wasn't afraid to express her disagreement with my decisions to him.

Yes, she was playing politics.

Political skill can also be a source of power in organizations, and employees need to pay as much attention to those with political power as they do those who have formal organizational power delegated to them.

A metaphor:

Picture the corporation as a large farm field in a country plagued by war, one that is filled with explosive charges. The formal rules system could be represented by some unexploded bombs, or sticks of dynamite wired up with detonators and ready to go off. It's obvious where the bombs and dynamite are, and obvious that if you mess around with them they will likely go off, blowing you to a million pieces.

Yet, every day people in companies around the world push their luck and fiddle with the formal rules system – doing things like falsifying expense reports, approving improper expenditures, or using company property for personal purposes. For example, every company of significant size has rules delegating power for purchasing decisions. Usually these are listed in dollar amounts and delegated based on title or organizational position. Violate those rules, and you're likely to get fired.

The informal rules system is more like a collection of Claymore mines, hidden under the dirt and often quite difficult for the average person to detect. An experienced soldier might be able to avoid the Claymores by knowing what to look for, but many still trip the explosive charges and are injured or killed. Soldiers that are going to survive usually step through a minefield carefully, no matter how experienced they are. For example, an employee who makes disparaging comments about his peers only when they aren't around to defend themselves might be violating the informal rules in some organizations. He isn't likely to be fired for it, unless the behavior is massively over the line, but his standing within the organization is still compromised.

If you trip a Claymore mine, it does damage but isn't always fatal – in this way, the informal rules might be more like a hidden firecracker. Tripping a hidden informal explosive causes some damage, but it definitely causes less carnage than detonating a five-hundred pound bomb or exploding twelve sticks of dynamite.

Organizations tend to be a bit more forgiving when the informal rules are violated, but they definitely still keep score. The mistake might kill you, or it might just give you some scars – ones you're likely to carry with you the rest of your time with that employer. Either way, there's plenty of incentive to avoid the Claymores, or even a well hidden mousetrap, for that matter.

Are the informal rules "politics" by themselves? Not really. "Politics" are an important set of techniques people use to navigate through the informal and formal rules present in their companies. In our metaphor, they are the Claymore mine detection and disarming equipment and methods. As we will see, it is possible to avoid employing politics yourself, but it is not possible to avoid being affected by it. The presence of the informal rules and their associated ambiguity, more than any other factor, create an environment that gives birth to and nurtures political life.

The main reason the informal rules exist is that formal rule systems are quite limited. Formal rules mainly deal with key decisions that have clearly defined right and wrong answers and address things like annual performance appraisals, financial decision making, and strategic direction setting. They usually don't extend down to the details of how people carry out their day-to-day tasks.

Why not?

Imagine trying to write the rulebook for how people are supposed to interact – you would need to think of every possible way people might need to relate to each other in the carrying out of their various duties, then come up with the rules bounding those interactions – ones that would produce the best results for the business. And don't forget about forbidding every undesirable behavior. The task would be enormous. Overwhelming. Then you'd have to get people to read it. And then enforce it! It's simply not practical. Informal rules fill these gaps between desired behavior and the formal rule systems.

The shortcomings of the informal rules are numerous – they are fuzzy, situational, often in flux, sometimes challenging to understand, unevenly applied, and can be manipulated by those skilled in the use of politics. These are some of the very reasons why people rail against them.

Informal rules systems may be maligned, but they are effective – sometimes ruthlessly so. And they support the overall business plan when correctly deployed.

The nature of politics in organizations:

The intention of politics is to change the way people perceive your, or someone else's, perception of *performance* in the context of the formal and informal rules. Making sure that people are aware you came in early today – politics. Letting your boss know a hated subordinate is badmouthing him – politics. Here *performance* is intended to mean the evaluation of how well the individual conforms to the formal and informal expectations of the organization.

Politics can be about either conformance to or violation of the formal rules, but it is much more often about the informal ones, where there is much more ambiguity. It revolves as much around perceptions of reality as it does the reality itself. If you think of the minefield metaphor again, politics is mostly about making others believe you didn't step on a Claymore, but the other guy did. Of course, this would be useless in war, because we can all see the real injuries. In the world of the large corporation, however, perception becomes reality. If enough people fervently believe something is true, it effectively is – particularly if the truth is difficult to tease out, or circumstantial evidence and personal prejudices agree with the perception.

For example, if there is a rumor running through the company that Joe is an alcohol abuser (reinforced by some real, observable data – like he is late to work every Monday morning), then he will be treated as if it were true. Joe could easily remain unaware this is the general perception, and as a result be unaware of a need to defend himself. Maybe Joe has to drop his kids off at school every Monday morning, or whatever the legitimate reason for his latJoe's political awareness and a campaign to change others' perceptions, he might as well be an alcoholic.

Political environments range from fairly straightforward and relatively benign to incredibly complex and ruthless. While it isn't possible to determine formulaically the savageness of a corporation's politics, we can at least look at some general tendencies:

A. **Organization size**: Generally the larger the organization, the more extensive the political minefield. With more mines it becomes easier to trip one accidentally. With larger organizations, an even larger part of a person's perceived performance is determined by gossip because of limited direct observation (see Chapter 2).

B. **Organization history**: There is a lot of inertia in companies. If the organization has had a high level of politics in the past, it's a good bet that it will continue (see Chapter 3).

C. **Extent of the formal rule system**: Politics seem to thrive in a vacuum. Where there is nothing written, there will be informal rules, and their associated higher level of politics. Clear and evenly applied written policies and procedures reduce, to some degree, the ambiguous environment where politics tends to reign (see Chapter 4).

D. **Style of the top executive**: Is the top executive hands-on (less politics), or more "strategic" or detached (more politics)? Does he or she tolerate or even encourage some of the most destructive political tactics such as bad mouthing or the setting up of internal competitions? Or does the top executive turn a blind eye to politics and simply claim "it doesn't happen here" (see Chapter 5)?

E. **The concentration of power players**: Power players (a term described in more detail later) are skilled at dropping their own mines in the field. They lay traps and exploit the political weaknesses of others. A large concentration of them usually means a more politically dangerous and destructive environment (see Chapter 6).

F. **Employee level in the company**: As people climb the ladder within the corporation, two things happen: it becomes harder to measure accurately their job performance (more ambiguity), and there are more people targeting them for political maneuvers. As a general rule being higher in the company means more political risk (see Chapter 7).

There is often a temptation to view informal rule systems in a strictly negative sense, but doing so ignores the fact that they exist as part of a disciplinary tools to regulate employee behavior. Informal systems help to get the employees within the organization to agree to decisions and to get them working toward common goals. If companies waited around for everybody to agree on their own, nothing would ever get done! And, as has already been discussed, developing formal power systems to do the same thing is impractical.

For the organization in total, informal rules are necessary, and politics, which are nurtured by the informal rules, are a necessary evil.

Would it be possible for a large corporation to avoid politics? Not a chance. Human nature, being what it is, will introduce politics around the formal and informal rules system. Politics work in the environment of opinion, perception, ambiguity, and opportunism. Politics are the willful attempt to bend perception for an individual's own purposes. If someone tells you their large organization has no politics, they are either disingenuous or simply ignorant.

Responses to the political environment:

If you accept my thesis that politics are present in virtually every large organization, the question is no longer politics *yes* or *no*. It really becomes how you respond to it.

Over the years, I've noted three different responses to corporate politics (one of which has two subsets). The first two are by far the most common.

Avoiders

These are typically people who either don't grasp organizational politics, or hate dealing with them with a passion. The latter appears to be more common than the former, and the reasoning expressed by avoider adherents seems to go as follows: "I hate this politics stuff so much that maybe if I just pretend it doesn't exist, it will go away. I should just put my head down, work hard, and maybe it won't impact me."

Much like the jury moralists on the TV reality show "Survivor," these folks never seem to understand the game or its rules. Trust me folks, if you want to win (meaning, successfully climb the corporate ladder), you have to at least learn the tools and tactics of corporate politics. To reach a high level in the company, you will almost certainly have to bend politics to your purposes. When avoiders are invariably "voted off the island," they are surprised, and they belligerently whine about how they were a victim of company politics, and how they always played (read: worked) the game "honestly," "fairly," and/or "morally."

If you are one of these people, you should probably resign yourself to working only on the bottom rungs of the corporate ladder. If you start climbing while ignoring the political environment, you're probably going to fall off the ladder, and probably in short order. When that happens, you will either be fired, or if you're an especially hard or effective enough worker, pigeon-holed. Ambition to climb, and political avoidance, don't go together. If you desire to have your cake and eat it too, shift to a smaller company, or start/buy your own (for more, see Chapter 8).

Neutrals

Neutrals generally understand the political realities present where they work and over time become adept at navigating through them. For personal reasons, often times ethical, they stop short of laying down mines of their own. That distinction belongs to our last class of politicians – the power players.

Neutrals often seem to find the political behaviors of others to be arbitrary, capricious, and to some degree, unfair. Because neutrals usually find politics distasteful, they often ignore them until they've already sustained some damage. But that doesn't describe all neutrals, some of whom could be very effective power players if they didn't find the power player class of tactics repugnant.

Anyone who wants to climb the corporate ladder needs to become at least a competent neutral, and the sooner the better. Even if it is distasteful, neutrals need to keep company politics in the front of their minds. Without constant vigilance, they are just as likely to become a victim as an avoider (for more, see Chapter 9).

Power players

Power players attempt to manipulate the political environment to their own or someone else's advantage. They are the ones laying traps and dropping additional mines for the rest of the company to trip over. When painted in such stark terms, it isn't hard to see why some neutrals reject power playing.

In reality, these classifications (avoider, neutral and power player) are artificial. I'm certain many neutrals engage in some political power playing once in a while. And power players aren't always obsessed with politics.

I have observed two types of power players who have widely varying approaches to manipulation of the political environment:

Street fighters: These power players are the terrorists of the corporation. They tend to be overt with their tactics, but can deposit some pretty powerful munitions – many of which are IED's (improvised explosive devices) targeted at specific individuals or small groups. Some street fighters can be ham-handed, and misunderstand or misestimate the skills of their targets. Over time street fighters make a lot of enemies, and there is often quiet cheering if they have their own tactics turned against them. Even though poetic justice seems to come to this type of power player more often than not, you should never under-estimate a street fighter – they can be perceptive, adept, and ruthless.

One street fighter I knew – the archetype of this classification, from my perception – systematically removed (through political gamesmanship) all of his peers, and it wasn't until he took aim at the CEO that he was terminated.

Maneuverers: Maneuverers are at the top of the political food-chain. In terms of our metaphor, they are the top explosives experts. They have the most advanced weapons-making and disguising skills and like to use them covertly. Unlike street fighters, maneuverers oftentimes have extensive networks of allies they can tap into to work their manipulations. It has been my observation that a significant concentration of maneuverers exist at the top levels of large corporations. Maneuverers tend to see politics more as a game they play to win, and they are

27

usually strategic in their actions. You might personally offend a maneuverer and suffer no consequences, if taking you out isn't in his or her best interests. But find yourself in a skilled maneuverer's sights, and your chances of long-term organizational survival are slim.

One of the best maneuverers I ever met managed to ambush me at a strategy session, offering a nasty critique of my strategy in front of the entire corporate staff. In this case he only acted after the CEO had already subtly indicated he would tolerate the attack. This maneuverer was so powerful, no one was willing to come to my aid and risk retribution.

Avoider, *neutral* or *power player*, the corporate political environment is going to impact you. Where you fall along the continuum may be governed by your personal sense of right and wrong, but ignorance of the politics of your organization will never work in your favor and certainly will not save you if you step on a mine. While there are literally scores, if not hundreds, of tactics, approaches, alliances, and strategies you can use to navigate through your employer's minefield, I've assembled some of the most common and most successful. In the balance of this chapter, you will find two lists of political tactics – one for skilled neutrals, the other for the budding power player (for more, see Chapter 10).

Ten basic skills needed by political neutrals:

These are the basic skills you need to survive in most political environments. I've tried to rank them roughly from most basic and safest to most complex and risky. If you are new to corporate politics, or can only force yourself to master a few of these skills, focus on the top ones first.

1. **Learn the Landscape.** It is critical to understand who are your allies and enemies. You should build connections with as many groups as possible – just don't give them the impression you fall into their camp exclusively. Knowing whose ox you may be goring is essential to making smart decisions. You must learn the positions the power players have staked out for themselves on important issues before you start expressing loud opinions. When in doubt, keep your mouth shut (see Chapter 11).

2. **Don't burn bridges, without thinking things through**. Maintain your relationships unless the consequences of doing so become very high, such as when your ally is about to be fired and is dragging you down with her. If you do have to burn a bridge, make sure you know your exposures. Sometimes you're forced to take sides in a dispute, but usually there are ways of doing this tactfully. Usually, but not always. When you can't successfully straddle an issue, make sure you know who you're taking on, and how they might come back at you. Anticipating the counter attack might give you time to prepare defenses, or might convince you not to burn the bridge in the first place (see Chapter 12).

3. **Figure out what is valued.** Most organizations have a set of behaviors they're looking for. You need to determine what they are (results, loyalty, sacrifice, or whatever), and how they're measured. If, for example, the organization values personal

sacrifice, and they measure it by how much vacation you don't take each year, then you need to manage perceptions along this dimension. It's surprising how many organizations seem to watch the clock and penalize employees that don't give extra time to the company. I'm not saying you have to comply, but knowing what you're giving up and what it might do to your potential to advance is essential to making wise decisions (see Chapter 13).

4. **Be careful about what you put in writing**, and think about how it could be used against you. Despite nearly continuous warnings to avoid emotional emails, I still read numerous politically damaging examples – often from people who should have known better. And don't think this admonition stops inside the company walls. If you write something obnoxious on Facebook, you can expect someone from work to find it and use it. Be particularly careful if you feel emotional about the topic you are writing about – emotional writing can often be picked apart or taken out of context by your enemies (see Chapter 14).

5. **Lend support before you need it**. Think of your political alliances in terms of a checkbook – when you support others, you add to the balance. When you need support, you are making a withdrawal. Of course, don't violate rule #2 by burning one bridge to lend support to someone else. Once you burn a bridge, virtually no amount of support will be enough to offset your past bad behavior (see Chapter 15).

6. **Make sure risks are tilted in your favor,** and limited in number. When you take risks, as you almost certainly will have to do at some point, do your best to make sure they will ultimately be recorded as wins. You might be able to survive one failure, but not three or four consecutively. A number of missed promises, or over estimates of your ability to perform, while small individually, can add up to one big bomb. When you have to take a big risk, make sure it's as close to a sure thing as possible. Better to renege on something you said previously than to be backed into taking on a big risk (see Chapter 16).

7. **Presentations count.** A lot. Top management will have limited opportunities to see you, learn about you, and assess your capabilities. Make sure you put your best foot forward when these opportunities come up. Master the subject matter (whatever it may be), take time to perfect your slides or other materials, and deliver it well. Bonus points are given for coming up with fresh or new ways to look at old problems (see Chapter 17).

8. **Don't hide bad news.** But be very careful about how you reveal it. I've found the "bad news sandwich" works the best with some good news on each side of the bad. And if you must make a confession, get the admission up front in a conversation. Senior management hates to feel like they had to "pry it out of you." It also helps if you have an action plan for how to handle any issues. Just make sure you're prepared to execute it (see Chapter 18).

9. **Don't badmouth your enemies**. Yes, you will probably have competitors or enemies, whether they are people you don't like, people who don't like you, or people who see you as an impediment to getting what they want. If you badmouth them, it is highly likely to get back to them, and you effectively raise your visibility as a target. That might not matter if they're an avoider, but if they're a power-playing street fighter – better watch out (see Chapter 19).

10. **Keep complaints to yourself.** If you're unhappy with some aspect of the company, go home and explain it to your spouse. Or better yet, your dog. Absolutely do not discuss it with other employees. Commiseration may feel good, but it is the stuff that starts rumors or offends others. Remember those things valued by your organization (tactic #3 above)? Well, being a disengaged employee isn't one of them. You can't afford to have anyone thinking you're disengaged. Of course, a light dose of criticism accompanied by a realistic plan to make improvements can get you far. Just be prepared to make it happen (see Chapter 20).

Ten advanced skills needed by aspiring power players:

These are the advanced skills you need to climb to the top of most large organizations. I've again tried to rank them roughly from simplest to most complex . They are all relatively risky. I recommend you focus on the top ones first. While it will help a neutral to be aware of these tactics, only engage in them once you've proven yourself skilled at managing the neutral tactics. Recognize that some of these tactics may be morally offensive to some employees, and be aware of your own moral compass as you consider active involvement in each.

11. **Actively manage your reputation**. You want to be seen as smart, hardworking, innovative, or whatever the company thinks is important. Be well aware of how you are seen by others, even if it means seeking the feedback of a keen observer (see next tactic on mentors). Work to correct any deficiencies (see Chapter 20).

12. **Cultivate a mentor**. Look for one who is a skilled politician of the type you aspire to be, as opposed to just somebody higher up the ladder (although being high up the ladder helps, too). Oddly, many skilled politicians, in the latter part of their careers, seem to develop a desire to help younger co-workers. Perhaps it's all the years of not being able to talk about their political maneuvering to anyone…(see Chapter 21)?

13. **Ask for what you want.** You can't expect the organization to figure out where you want to go and put you there – at least not without some prodding. Ambition is generally admired as long as you don't appear to be a threat to the person you are talking to. Carefully make your long-term desires known in a benign fashion (see Chapter 22).

14. **Set the bar credibly low.** Make no mistake about it, hitting your targets is important in almost every organization. How the target is set, however, can sometimes be completely disconnected from

reality. Eighty percent of your wins or losses will be determined not by how hard, smart, or fast you work, but instead by where the bar is set. Managers are taught in business school to set high targets for their subordinates. They later learn to build in a cushion in their own targets, and push down blame. So take every opportunity to make sure you score wins rather than losses by influencing the setting of targets at a reasonable level – the lower the better (see Chapter 25).

15. **Provide some original thinking.** Original thinking can greatly enhance your reputation. While what's valued by corporations does vary, I've never seen one yet that didn't highly value having smart and creative people on the team. "Smart" can sometimes neutralize, or at least reduce, other negative perceptions. The ability to introduce new ideas to the company is critical to being seen as "smart" (avoiding stupid mistakes helps, too!). The ideas need not be completely novel, just new to the company. And the best part about it is – these ideas don't have to necessarily go anywhere (see Chapter 24).

16. **Promote yourself.** This requires the lightest of touches. It's a fine line between tooting one's own horn and being seen as an obnoxious self-promoter. One of the best ways to do this that I've seen is to discuss one of your successes, but credit the other people involved in making it a win. It looks generous and still gets the point across. Better if you can enlist someone else to promote you. This can be done explicitly in an agreement

of mutual support, or can just evolve through a series of *quid pro quo* cheerleading (see Chapter 25).

17. **Distance yourself from failure.** There's an old adage that "success has many fathers, but failure is an orphan." If only that were true. Many large organizations seem to have an almost pathological need to identify and punish the person(s) responsible for failures. As soon as you see a ship is sinking, my advice is to be the first rat to jump (see Chapter 26).

18. **Expect betrayal.** Business relationships are often relationships of convenience – and it may become convenient to sacrifice you at some point. To reduce this risk, you need to deepen your relationships with some of your best and strongest supporters. Get to know them as people outside of the work environment, and build bonds of friendship. Even then, be prepared that you may be cast off by an ally when you are in greatest need (see Chapter 27).

19. **Invest in scapegoats**. Whenever possible, try to insert someone between yourself and high-risk projects or tasks. That way, if failure occurs on the project, that person can be sacrificed. It might not save you in every case, but I've seen the technique used time and again by senior managers. This technique is perhaps the most morally repugnant political behavior, and regardless of advice to the contrary, I could never personally bring myself to utilize scapegoats. That being said, it does work if it is within your moral comfort zone (see Chapter 28).

20. **Use sparingly, use strategically.** Power player tactics are often seen as obnoxious or offensive by the organization at large. Overindulgence in them can make you a target by itself. Sparing use and covert use will get you much further than craftlessly lashing about (see Chapter 29).

Conclusion:

Corporate politics are endemic in large organizations, and they are an outgrowth of both human nature and the necessary fuzziness and gaps surrounding the formal and informal rules.

People react differently in response to the environment. Some fail to grasp it, or are in denial about it (avoiders). Others understand, but elect only to act defensively (neutrals). And a few embrace and thrive in the political environment (power players).

Out of scores of tactics, ten common tactics used by neutrals were highlighted, and another ten were described that are employed by power players alone. While most people seem to be able to stomach the basic tactics, the power player tactics contain distasteful lying, deceit, and betrayal that clearly aren't for everyone.

I spent many years in senior management positions in large corporations, and was a neutral. I could never get comfortable with the moral implications of using most of the advanced techniques. I did, however, benefit greatly by being able to recognize them – oftentimes to prepare my defenses, if nothing else. I observed the power player tactics used successfully time and again by peers, bosses, and select subordinates.

If the advanced techniques bother you to the extreme, you may need to give up your dream of being a chief executive someday. I've never worked for a CEO who didn't utilize these tactics adeptly.

Section 2 – The Corporate Environment

Chapter 2 – How Large is Large?

When I began my career at General Motors Corporation thirty years ago, it was an organization with more than half a million employees. And it was, as you might expect, a wildly political organization. There were corporate politics, divisional politics, departmental politics, and everything in between. I wouldn't say career success was unrelated to skill and capability, but to move upward, you needed to capture the right attention – by being at the right place, working on the right project, and by having the right sponsors. Even then, it was tough.

I eventually left General Motors after realizing that unless something completely out of the ordinary occurred – like the entire divisional leadership team quit, or I somehow became personal friends with the CEO – I had little to no chance to advance significantly. In an organization of such huge dimension, even getting into the political games was no simple feat.

I've worked in three other large companies: one with tens of thousands of employees, one with a few thousand employees, and another with a few hundred. Presently I have partial ownership of a company with only fifteen employees, and it is only there that I've seen politics fade into unimportance – and even then, only because my partner and I are not interested in pinning guilt on someone for every problem we experience. Even there, however, there is still a bit of politically motivated behavior. For example, we just recently discussed the need one employee had never to be blamed for anything that went wrong – quite probably motivated by concerns it would impact her standing with those higher up in the organization.

All the larger companies were highly politicized organizations, and there was no question, in my personal experience, that the larger the organization, the more politics mattered. At least part of the reason for this may be the concentration of power and decision making at the top. When one person's edicts control so many fates – without adequate knowledge of the individuals, and little patience to get to the bottom of what is going on before making pronouncements – people are going to try to manipulate outcomes. If the CEO is passing judgment on all salary increases, for example, and can't possibly personally measure the performance of employees involved – well, there's going to be a hefty load of politics.

Another cause is the ambiguity present in larger organizations. With fine division of labor and multiple hand-offs at every level of the company, there is a lot of "white space" that seemingly is no one's and everyone's responsibility. This is fertile ground for politics to take root.

So how big does a company need to become for politics to loom largely on the employee's radar? How large does the entity need to be for skill at politics to be a requirement for success? Or even survival?

It depends.

It depends on a number of factors, many of which are covered in the next couple of chapters. In general, other than just sheer size, the key factor appears to involve the bandwidth and preferences of the company's leader.

If the CEO is hands on – involved in the day-to-day activities of the business, and closely watches the behaviors of a large cross-section of the employees – the company could have as many as a couple hundred employees before politics starts to become critical. If the CEO is disengaged – failing to follow the daily ebb and flow of the company – the organization could have significant politics with only a couple dozen employees.

When the "wool" can be effectively pulled over the leader's eyes through political machinations, a politicized company is highly likely. And that includes pretty much any organization we would classify as large, mid-sized, and even quite a few that would be called small.

Chapter 3 – How does History Impact Politics?

Old habits die hard. At least in corporations, they usually do.

If you've ever worked in a large corporation, you've probably experienced resistance to change. I like to call it human inertia, borrowing a bit from Newton's Second Law (a body in motion tends to stay in motion…). People are conditioned to keep doing those things that have worked for them in the past. So it stands to reason that if you're joining an organization that has had a high level of politics in the past, it will likely stay that way for a while – regardless of what anyone (including the CEO) says. And if the organization had limited politics in the past, it is likely to stay that way, too. At least for a while.

Certainly the chief executive (and to a lesser degree, other high-level executives) has an influence over the company's direction – he/she sets strategy, maybe refines the mission and values, and over enough time, may even change the political profile of the organization.

But in my experience, it happens infrequently, and very slowly.

Sometimes organizational inertia is called "culture." I personally dislike applying the term here, because "culture" has become one of those heavily-overused, fuzzy business terms. Sometimes when a person rails against a company's negative "culture," they are really railing against a highly politicized environment which has been self-sustaining for a long period of time.

Suppose a firm's last chief executive (who was in place for twenty-five years, for argument's sake), was a detached, high flying strategist who allowed freewheeling politics to overrun the organization. When this chief executive retires and is replaced by a hands-on CEO who hates politics, how long does it take to change the underlying environment?

The answer is – a long time. And it will likely be a very painful period. The old system is so deeply imbedded in the behaviors of the people, it has become self-perpetuating. The survivors of the old regime, particularly those near the top, flourished in the former, highly political environment. In their world, certain tactics and political maneuvering became a part of their management toolbox. Techniques that previously produced successes are very hard for people to let go of, particularly since the old system continues to function despite what the new boss may be demanding.

Unfortunately, for the current team, the quickest way to change the environment would be to change out the people. Since it isn't practical to fire everyone, what actually happens in most cases is a few people are sacrificed during the transition, and change plods along very slowly.

In one of my positions as a division president, I came into an organization that was highly politicized due to the arbitrary nature of my predecessor's decision making process (or lack thereof). He would make frequent judgments about strategies, projects, and people, based on scant information – relying on his "gut feeling." Not surprisingly, this produced a highly political organization.

It took several years for me to change how things were done within the division, and it eventually required me to release several members of the senior management team – not because they weren't talented, but because they just couldn't seem to figure out that the ground rules had changed.

Once politics are introduced to an organization, however, it doesn't seem to take very long for the associated behaviors to take root. This may be a result of people with experience in other politicized organizations quickly recognizing what they are seeing, and knowing that continued survival, or eventual success, are dependent on getting with the new game.

Chapter 4 – How do Formal and Informal Rules Relate?

There are written formal rules, policies, and structures in corporations that are pretty straightforward and reasonably clear to everyone involved. And there is a second set of expectations for behavior that takes over where the formal stuff leaves off.

You don't put fake expenses on your expense reports. Everybody working for a corporation already understands this. In most companies it's written down (a formal rule), along with the consequences for violating the policy. If it weren't written down, there would still be a prohibition against faking your expense reports. Such a ban would just be part of the informal rules. As an informal rule, it would be open to a lot more interpretation and argument. Is that movie you rented in your hotel room a legitimate expense? How about the massage? If you brought a sack lunch on the plane, can't you just charge the company for the burger you would have eaten? And so on, and so forth.

The entire collection of written, behavior-regulating policies, are referred to in this book as the **formal rules** of the corporation. Formal rules tend to focus on things like spending authorization, approval processes, personal behaviors (like vacations, tardiness, allowable travel behaviors), organizational structure (who reports to whom), and performance measurement (that damned appraisal process).

Extensive though this collection may seem, it is always much smaller in scope than the vast collection of unwritten, behavior-regulating rules, which I have called the **informal rules** of the corporation. People sometimes refer to the informal rules as the "culture" of the organization (although "culture" – as mentioned in the previous chapter – is one of those overused business terms that, like an unsharpened knife, has lost its edge).

The **informal rules**, like a gas, fill the gaps around the formal rules. And there are usually some big gaps. Since the informal rules are fuzzier, unwritten, situational, and subjective, they foster political behavior. In other words, the less that is documented, the more political behavior the organization is likely to experience.

If there's no formal dress code, you learn that jeans are only acceptable on Friday by observing or asking. Friday jeans day is an informal rule. It becomes a point of politics when an employee points out (usually to someone in management) how another person has crossed the line by wearing them on Thursday.

Informal rules can be quite subtle and are often confusing, and sometimes need to be interpreted on the fly. When I was a new employee, I suffered a reprimand for failing to place a warning call to my boss on Friday prior to our regular Monday morning staff meeting. Warnings over bad news were expected, and I learned that particular informal rule the hard way – by violating it.

The formal and informal rules provide the backdrop for the politics of the organization. **Politics** are about figuring out what is permitted by the rules, what is outside of them, and managing the *perception* of your behavior (or that of others) in that context. Perception is at least as important as reality, because your compliance with the norms is only important as seen through the eyes of the people that control your future. Their perception (accurate or otherwise) becomes their reality, and they will treat you as such.

Playing politics is simply the manipulation of perceptions – either perceptions about yourself or someone else.

Organizations with fewer clear formal rules tend to have more politics, and usually more politics playing. This occurs because of the ambiguity surrounding the informal rules which tend to dominate many of the day-to-day activities of the business. More ambiguity results in more opportunity to push the limits of the rules, which creates more openings to manipulate perceptions.

When you hear someone say, "We don't want too many rules, because they hinder creativity," what they are really saying is, "We let the informal rules take care of that stuff, despite their inherent messiness."

Chapter 5 – The Style of the Top Dog Matters

Politics in the corporation (or politics anywhere, for that matter) revolves around *perceptions* rather than reality. If you are politically active, then you are engaged in managing those perceptions – either perceptions of you (which is usually viewed as acceptable), or of someone else (often viewed as underhanded, unless done in a positive way).

Why do we need to be worried about perceptions? Why can't we just rely on our supervisors and those higher up to know the reality of our behaviors and our performance? Why isn't life in the corporation a perfect meritocracy?

Because corporations are run by human beings, and being human means having limitations in capacity, knowledge, perception, and judgment. Management isn't about being perfect – it's about being good enough to get it right most of the time. Being perfect would require so much capacity that a company would collapse under the weight of its own overhead.

I've already discussed the practical impossibility in large corporations of the person at the top understanding and being able to pass accurate judgment over a hundred (let alone thousands) of employees. But the CEO does have a substantial bearing on the way employees are perceived in the corporation, and the most senior executives have a hand in it as well. The senior management world revolves around their perceptions of the abilities and successes of the employees working further down in the organization – perceptions that are often built on very limited personal interaction, and a smattering of comments by others whose judgments are trusted.

CEO's vary in the way they approach gathering this information and passing judgment on their lower-level subordinates. Once an employee is written off by the top dog, there is often little that can be done to salvage their careers.

When perception is that important, and the connection to data is distant, you can be sure there will be plenty of politics going on.

CEO behaviors that tend to increase an organization's level of politics include:

- Stays detached from day-to-day operations.
- Takes the word of other senior executives about employees who don't work for them.
- Makes snap judgments about employees whom he or she doesn't know well.
- Is unclear or vague in opinions or direction.
- Allows employees to operate with incorrect assumptions.
- Doles out substantial consequences for mistakes (commonly referred to as "holding people accountable").
- Acts as though every problem has a cause with a person's name attached to it.

- Scapegoats, and/or tolerates scapegoating.

I'm sure there are other behaviors that can contribute to a wild political environment. (If you have any piercing insights, please email them to me!). And I'm not saying these behaviors are all necessarily bad. In fact, research shows that some of them correlate well to superior organizational performance. I'm simply saying they result in increased playing of politics in the company.

On the other hand, there are other top executive behaviors that will reduce the level of politics:

- Adheres to the formal rules system, even if painful (as in forcing an unpleasant action like firing a critical employee) in the short term.
- Is hands-on, well aware of the day-to-day happenings within the organization, particularly those related to employee performance.
- Respects an immediate supervisor's evaluations of their subordinates.
- Is clear and consistent in direction.
- Is slow to judge employees further down the ladder.
- Takes personal responsibility for mistakes and failures.
- Believes that people usually *try* to do a good job, and acknowledges that some issues cannot be overcome by a simple swap out of people.
- Is aware of who on the management team is using obnoxious political tactics (scapegoating, pushing high-risk assignments onto others, blaming) to advance their career, and swiftly removes them from the team.

The top executive (along with the company's history) sets the tone for politics within the corporate environment.

While the CEO can't necessarily control all politics, or rid the organization of them, he or she can communicate intolerance for some of the more egregious tactics. Ambiguity and snap judgments are the friend of corporate politics, and certainty and consistency are their enemy. The CEO that focuses on building a safe, data-based, decision-driven organization and consistently adheres to his or her own rules will slowly be able to reduce (but not eliminate) the politics going on in their organization.

Chapter 6 – Power Players Beget more Power Players

An obvious point, but one worth stating: the more people playing politics in the organization, the more politicized the overall environment becomes.

More people playing politics means more attempted management of perceptions, more injured innocent bystanders, and more need to continuously monitor the way one is seen by others.

Once *power players* – those people who manipulate the perceptions of others in the organization using politics – make a successful appearance in the organization, increasing politics becomes a foregone conclusion, particularly when the power players are high in the organization.

Power players act by taking aim at other people – either overtly or covertly – and causing them problems or sometimes cheerleading for them. A power player might maneuver targeted individuals onto high-risk projects, then discredit them when the project fails. Or they might take advantage of a violation of the informal rules of the company to run down the reputation of a perceived competitor in an attempt to get them fired. Or they might help a supporter by acting as their promoter, making sure key decision-makers recognize the supporter's supposed worth to the organization.

The higher the power player is up the corporate ladder, the more likely it is that person will successfully be able to accomplish these manipulations. And the more likely they will be a skilled politician as well. That's how power players raise the stakes for everyone in the company, driving increased politics-playing by all.

What are the possible responses to the power player? People can either avoid them, ally with them, or take them on. When employees develop their political skills in order to team up with or take on a power player, it further raises the intensity for everyone.

Definitely a "one bad apple can spoil the whole barrel" scenario.

When assessing the level of political activity at a corporation, it is edifying to study the most active high-level power players. Are they adept? Are most members of the senior team also power players? The higher the concentration of power players, the higher up they are, and the more active, the more likely it is that politics will be running rampant throughout the organization.

Chapter 7 – Politics and Position on the Ladder

The higher up the corporate ladder you climb, the more important understanding and playing politics is to success and survival.

Why, you might ask, would this be true? There are three primary reasons:

1. The higher up the ladder you go, the more difficult it is to determine whether an employee is performing. Factors such as changes in market conditions, performance of subordinates, validity of assumptions, and trade-offs between different strategic options all tend to muddy the waters. When you can't easily gauge the person's output, there is a tendency to rely on watching what they do – except senior managers rarely have the time to watch it all. As a result, performance perceptions are often established by what others say, and the small amount of direct observation that actually occurs becomes extremely important. This produces a fertile environment for cultivating the playing of politics. Politics is all about developing and protecting perceptions of how you

are doing, and potentially manipulating perceptions about others.

2. There is a higher concentration of politicians at the upper levels in the company, and they tend to have more skill. I'm not sure why this is true – a Darwinian survival characteristic, perhaps? You need political skills at higher levels, if for no other reason than to protect yourself from the manipulations of the skilled power players found there. An individual contributor who has few enemies can probably get by at most companies while ignoring politics. Senior managers won't survive being apolitical, no matter how nice they are, or how well they perform. There are just too many sharks in those waters.

3. At higher levels you become a bigger target for the political machinations of others. This tends to happen for a couple of reasons – senior managers are more useful targets of manipulation, because they generally command more power. They also have less time available to know intimately the performance of others in the organization, thus making them more vulnerable to manipulation. Some senior managers end up surrounded by yes-men/women who convince them their opinions and beliefs are always correct, while at the same time subtly attempting to manipulate perceptions. This seems to happen to the chief executive fairly frequently.

High on the ladder, politics become thicker, more ruthless, and impossible to ignore. If you have interest in climbing the corporate ladder, recognize you will quickly become embroiled in this world.

Chapter 8 – Avoiders

We can break people into three different groups by looking at how they respond to politics in an organization. The types are: 1) avoiders – those who ignore the political environment, 2)neutrals – those who recognize the existence of politics, but don't embrace the entire toolkit of political tactics for one reason or another, and 3) power players – those who engage in any and all political tactics. Although I recognize many people will fall somewhere between these classifications, it is much easier to draw distinctions between different behaviors by thinking of people as falling strictly in these buckets.

Avoiders either aren't aware of the political environment, or they're in denial about what their senses reveal. There is also a special class of avoiders – voluntary avoiders – who hate dealing with politics so much they aren't willing to participate. I'll discuss each in turn.

1. *Those who aren't aware of the political environment:* These people are so imperceptive of human interactions that they don't pick up on enough of what's going on in the organization to see the political landscape. Perhaps these people have very low awareness of the emotions of others (sometimes called low emotional intelligence). The unaware are likely to make huge and very obvious mistakes

when faced with political situations. They will leave other employees scratching their heads at times.

2. *Those who are in denial:* Some people, despite good emotional perception, pretend that there are no politics going on in the organization. I'm not sure why this happens, and I've only seen it a few times. It almost seems their image of other people in the organization is out of sync with the political behavior going on. They can't seem to align the two. Something has to give, and it ends up being the political reality.

3. *Those who hate politics:* This is a moralistic position, as opposed to one related to perceptive skills. In most of the situations when I've seen this behavior, the argument made is to completely eschew politics because they are "unfair" or "undemocratic." I've seen this happen most often with young people that are relatively new to the workforce, but it does show up to some degree across the entire spectrum. The attitude is similar to the following hypothetical conversation: Father: "Son, nobody is going to take you seriously in the corporate world with that tongue piercing and facial tattoo." Son: "That's stupid, unfair, and just wrong!" The point is, the voluntary avoider's claims of "unfairness" don't change a thing. The political reality still exists whether they elect to participate or not.

A variant of this last group is the rather sizable sub-group that believes only performance should matter in corporate progression and reward. They fervently believe politics and its skillful playing shouldn't be a factor in someone's success or failure. Unfortunately, their faith that performance can be the only basis for judgment is entirely misplaced. Other than the most elementary jobs, performance itself is open to interpretation. Managers are regularly called upon to compare apples to oranges when it comes to performance, even if the level of achievement is reasonably cut and dry. Just measuring performance is a combination of data, opinion, bias, perspective, and emotion. Keeping politics and its influence out of this "performance soup" is an unrealistic expectation.

The advice I've offered to avoiders in the past is this: work for a small company, start your own business, or be satisfied with not climbing above the first couple of rungs of the corporate ladder. Is it fair? No. Is it reality? You bet.

Chapter 9 – Neutrals

The fuzziest category of responses to the corporate political environment is definitely those of the neutrals.

There are a few characteristics that define a neutral, but many of them take on some behaviors of both avoiders and power players. Unlike avoiders, they are generally aware of and understand the political environment. Neutrals are typically willing to engage in *defensive* tactics, but usually not *offensive* ones. There can be several reasons for this reluctance: they may not understand how the *offensive* tactics work, they may conclude those tactics are too risky for them to employ, or they find them morally reprehensible. I'll talk at greater length about *defensive* tactics in later chapters, but for now simply understand that *defensive* political tactics involve managing your own image and the perceptions about you. When the tactics begin slipping into altering perceptions about others, you're going on the *offensive*. These can then be broken into two groups – *positive offensive* tactics (and alas, there aren't many of these), where the user is trying to improve someone else's image, and *negative offensive* tactics. Generally, neutrals never engage in negative offensive tactics.

For example, let's say (as was the case with one of my real-world employers) you recognize your level of commitment is being measured by the number of hours you spend at work.

An avoider would simply ignore this reality – either voluntarily or in ignorance.

An adept neutral would make sure that whenever the boss was watching, he was putting in long hours. The neutral might also cut out early, or take an extra-long lunch break, if he knew the boss was out of town. (Doing so being more a question of personal integrity than political type). The neutral might also engage in conversations about how little of their vacation they used, or how much time they had to spend working at home over the weekend.

A power player would take this one or more steps further – he or she might identify an organizational rival, and then devise a clever way to make sure the boss knew that person wasn't as committed. The power player would find a way to expose that three-hour lunch, or the fact that the rival was playing solitaire for an hour on the computer each day.

Neutrals run the gamut from ham-handed to skilled, just like power players. I've personally witnessed some pretty poorly executed self-promotion over the years by political neutrals. Others have proven themselves to be extremely skilled politicians, they simply limit the tactics they will voluntarily employ.

Neutrals remain neutrals and don't venture onward to becoming power players for three reasons:

1. They might be unaware of power player tactics. I believe this actually applies to very few people. If someone is ignorant of *offensive* tactics, they would generally be classified as an avoider. I can't rule out the possibility that a few neutrals might know

just enough to utilize some neutral tactics poorly, but this is rather rare.

2. They recognize that power player techniques are quite risky -- too risky, in their opinion. There is little question that offensive tactics are more difficult to get right and more likely to create problems if they go wrong. Some individuals probably do the math and decide becoming a power player is simply not for them.

3. They see many of the things power players do as *wrong* or *unfair*. I personally fell in this category during my career. While I had no problem trying to improve my own image, there was something that felt *wrong* about trying to alter someone else's negatively.

Sometimes neutrals fail to recognize a political reality, and other times they may try a power player tactic or two. I estimate the vast majority of corporate professionals and managers are neutrals. Unfortunately for them, adept power players typically rise to the top rungs of the ladder, and they often do it on the backs of political neutrals.

Chapter 10 – Power Players

If you aren't an avoider or a neutral, then you actively try to promote or undermine others in the organization. That makes you a power player.

As mentioned previously, power players come in two types – *street fighters* and *maneuverers*. They are very different in their approach, but both essentially try to accomplish the same thing – change perceptions about others, rather than just themselves. The difference is in the methods they employ to do this – a street fighter is overt, while a maneuverer is covert.

Maneuverers are more numerous than street fighters for reasons I'll describe momentarily. To be a successful maneuverer, one must be keenly aware of the existing rules of the corporation (formal and informal), as well as who has power. The maneuverer must be able to see how rules and holders of power can be manipulated to produce an advantage.

The work of a maneuverer is subtle. In many cases, the intended target is unaware they are the subject of a political play. In other situations, the target may be aware, but isn't sure which maneuverer might be behind the tactics. In almost all cases, the target is unable to do much of anything to stop the scheme from playing out.

Many maneuverers play politics a little like a stock broker plays the market – market goes up, I win; market goes down, I win. They back their targets into a position where they are faced with a bad choice and a worse one. Sometimes the objective directly helps the maneuverer – as when scapegoating, for example. If the maneuverer successfully identifies someone to take the blame for a mistake, then the blame doesn't fall to them. Sometimes the objective indirectly benefits the maneuverer – the removal or discrediting of a competitor or opponent. For example, I saw a skilled maneuverer pin the blame for a corporate gaff (the public release of some sensitive information) on a critical subordinate of his main rival. When the subordinate was fired, his competitor was significantly weakened.

The higher-level positions in most large corporations are loaded with maneuverers. This is why some of the craziest political battles occur in the rarefied air of the executive offices. In the crowded middle rungs of the organization, maneuverer skills help executives ascend the corporate ladder. The maneuverer toolbox contains both offensive and defensive weapons which help rising stars on the way up.

The primary reason there is a higher population of maneuverers than street fighters is because covert activity carries with it lower risks. If a target doesn't know who is behind the political play, it's hard to fight back. Even if the target does grasp what's going on, it's often impossible to do anything about it, as the source of the tactic is not clear.

Many maneuverers seem to admire a game well played by other maneuverers in the organization. I've seen the evidence of this behind closed doors – in one instance the entire political playing field was well understood by the

CEO, and he and his right-hand man actually expressed approval of a particularly skillful maneuverer's behavior. They also blamed the hapless target for being "stupid." Maneuverers rarely seem to have similar admiration for street fighters.

Street fighters are a rare breed, and I don't think they are necessarily present in all organizations. A street fighter openly identifies targets and goes after them. The best example of a street fighter in my career successfully removed several competitors from the organization. Surprisingly, his boss, a skillful maneuverer in his own right, tolerated the situation. It was only when this street fighter went after the boss himself that he was removed from the company.

The primary reason street fighters are so rare? They make a lot of enemies. When the world is lined up against you, any small misstep can be the key to a downfall. Street fighters generally have a large number of other politically active people just waiting to exploit any mistake.

I don't know of any large organization headed by a street fighter. I suspect the incongruity between the demeanor expected by boards and shareholders and the street fighter's overt tactics make it difficult for them to reach the corner office.

While maneuverers develop their skills over time, street fighters appear to be born. I don't know how else we could explain the existence and persistence of street fighters without suspecting there was something innate driving their aggressiveness. My experience definitely show maneuverers are more successful.

Just like the distinctions between avoiders, neutrals, and power players, I'm talking about the power players as if there was only a bilateral choice – maneuverer or street fighter. In reality, some maneuverers occasionally engage in street fighter tactics. Street fighters are capable of subtle maneuvering as well. There are undoubtedly many grades between the two extremes.

Subsequent chapters will detail some of the most common tactics used by neutrals and power players. Doing so will help further distill the differences in approach, and how the various roles shape the political environment of corporations.

Section 3 – Tactics for Neutrals

Chapter 11 – Learn the Landscape

The first and most important political skill any neutral or power player needs to master is the ability to understand alliances and important hot buttons issues those alliances are built upon. These structures can be hard to ferret out, and they may change on a fairly regular basis. Without an understanding of who is connected to which issues, you will be doomed to blunder around the political scene like a bull in a china shop.

Sometimes unlikely people may have substantial political power. In one organization, the seventy-year-old secretary to the long-retired chairman was the wrong person to cross. In others, personal friendships between the CEO and low-level employees can give those employees political influence far above that which would be expected based on formal position alone.

Political relationships are sometimes built on real friendships, but oftentimes they are arrangements of convenience. Because of that, you can't just rely on who eats lunch with whom (although that's certainly something to take note of) when trying to sort out the landscape.

Most organizations have a handful of hot-button issues that are central points along which battle lines are drawn. The web of relationships around those hot-buttons is a central feature of the political environment. For example, in one organization, there was a significant disagreement over how to integrate a recent acquisition. This became a key hot-button around which alliances were configured.

To be successful, you must figure out your company's hot-button issues, and then learn how the key executives are arranged around them. Once you have it all "mapped out," you'll know the organization's political landscape.

Another example might help – this one a significant disagreement over centralized control versus decentralization. In the company, the battle over this issue was played out in the way the purchasing organization was structured. Some people's positions were fairly predictable – divisional operations VP's didn't want a centralized structure, as it made their jobs more difficult. Senior corporate management found a centralized structure more appealing, because it was theoretically more cost-efficient. But there were a couple of key senior corporate players who felt the decentralized structure led to better accountability and was worth the price.

In this example, the new Vice President of Corporate Procurement made a lot of mistaken assumptions about who was on each side of the issue. By doing so, the VP alienated potential allies, and solidified opposition. She failed to master this first tactic of corporate politics – knowing the landscape.

Yes, it's complicated. So how do you figure out the issues and connections driving business? First, you must be patient. It takes time to sort through an organization's political landscape, and until you do, you're likely to blunder badly should you try to step into the fray.

Identifying the hot buttons is usually the simplest step. There won't be more than a dozen of them, and they tend to be the items people frequently talk about when having casual conversations. As you go along, gather information about who is on each side of the issues. Try to base your determination mostly on what they say and do, and not whom they are friends with or their job title. While those pieces of information can be indicators, they can also mislead you. One of the Procurement VP's biggest mistakes was to assume all the division presidents were in favor of a fully decentralized structure – which wasn't correct.

Next, start to look for patterns. People who tend to be in lockstep on most hot-button issues are probably allies. This will help you identify the major political camps and their captains. Bear in mind the picture isn't static. People, particularly fringe players and those who don't find an issue either threatening or compelling, may shift their positions and alliances frequently.

The only way I know to short-cut this process is to develop a mentor who will share their own observations about the political landscape. This is much faster as you don't need to figure out all the details, but it does mean putting your full trust in one person. I attempted to do this once with disastrous results – the "mentor" passed along sensitive information I revealed directly to my boss. Be absolutely sure of your mentor before you get overly committed to this path.

And whatever you do, keep your trap shut until you are fully aware of the implications of what you say. Expressing your opinions strongly before you know where others stand is dangerous.

You'll have no idea whom you might turn into an enemy.

Chapter 12 – Don't Burn Bridges (Without Thinking Things Through)

Conventional wisdom tells you to never burn bridges, but can you really go through your career straddling every issue so as not to offend anyone?

I doubt it. I certainly wasn't able to do so, not that I had set the avoidance of bridge burning as a goal.

Many people allow themselves to be drawn into unnecessary political battles, and in the process they burn bridges (i.e. permanently damage relationships) without really thinking things through.

So rather than offering the traditional counsel to never burn a bridge, I simply say this – know the stakes. If you do decide to destroy a relationship, know exactly what that means in the short and the long term. While in most cases, you can find a way to dance around the issue without offense, once in a while, you will have to take a stand.

Imagine you're on a company's senior staff, and an acquisition is being reviewed. You know the CEO is going to ask every person in the room to give their opinion (a go/no-go vote) of the proposed deal at the end of the review. A peer in another division is advocating the deal, and you can tell from the discussion that the CFO is adamantly opposed. What do you do?

Chances are, you aren't going to be able to straddle this one – it would hard to be in favor and opposed to the deal at the same time. You certainly can try to be as inoffensive as possible, perhaps by outlining the good and bad points of both positions before you vote. But the fact of the matter is, you have a good chance of alienating the person you vote against – either the CFO or the peer.

Of course there are questions of fact and questions of politics both at play. The questions of fact might surround the financial projections, the integration plans, and all the other things you've learned to ask about in school or on the job. These details are normally thoroughly discussed during the review.

The questions of politics aren't typically discussed. Such questions might be – *who is more important to my future – my peer or the CFO? Is my peer the next COO of the company, or is he a lame duck on his way out?* It is also important to understand who is allied with each party. *Is the CEO listening intently to the CFO and nodding, or is he quietly rolling his eyes when a challenge is issued? Which way is your most important political ally leaning?* To answer these questions you must carefully observe word, tone, and body language.

Once you have the stakes figured out, then what? You must know what you stand to win and lose based on any position you might take. In our example, if you know the deal is going to be killed because the CEO is aligned with his financial guy, you might choose to vote in favor of the deal, currying favor with your peer. Anytime you're on the losing side of an issue, you're less likely to burn a bridge. On the other hand, if you know the CFO is a vindictive

71

grudge holder, you might choose to vote with him. It's all a question of properly reading the situation and forecasting the political implications of your actions.

Of course, in my example I'm assuming there isn't a clear-cut correct answer. Sometimes the facts of the situations speak for themselves. Acquisition decisions tend to reflect opinions about the future, rather than facts, but plenty of controversial subjects can be settled with data. If there is a clear, factually correct answer, follow it, regardless of political ramifications. Otherwise, you run the risk of looking like an idiot.

Once you've decided to take a position that will burn a bridge, think through your vulnerabilities. Does the person I'm alienating (or one of her allies) know something about me that could be damaging? How might they counter-attack, or try to get me out of the way? What can I do to prevent that from being successful? Once you've sorted through these details, you might just want to reconsider taking the bridge-burning position.

Success in politics means anticipating, thinking things through, and being a couple of steps ahead of your opponents. Burning bridges puts you squarely into the political fray, so go there only when you're sure you're ready.

Chapter 13 – Figure Out What's Valued

Know the behaviors, traits, and accomplishments that are valued by the organization (or, in most cases, the CEO and/or senior managers). This may seem obvious, but I've seen it violated many times.

Don't waste time developing a performance record along dimensions that don't matter. For example, if your organization doesn't value creative skills, don't expend your efforts showing everyone how creative you are. Conversely, if your organization values meeting confrontations head on, you're helping your cause by conforming.

But you can't do either if you're unaware of the characteristics that are valued.

Most organizations have certain behaviors they *say* are important. One company I worked for claimed to select managers based on passion, integrity, continuous improvement, and the ability to produce results. This list was only partially accurate – I would dispute the part about "the ability to produce results," as it seemed to mean "the ability to achieve budget regardless of circumstances or mistaken assumptions." And I would have to reject the "continuous improvement" aspect entirely. Based on my personal observations and experience, there are several other characteristics that belong on the list – some of which I detail below.

The point is, companies often say one thing and do another. Characteristics that are stated as valuable are sometimes aspirational – they represent the way the company would *like* to value its people, not how it actually *does* value them. There are hints about what's really important, but it's hardly enough to be definitive. The only way to figure out what's truly valued is to observe and discuss with others (close allies only).

It definitely matters who's providing the critiques – the CEO, higher-level employees, and obvious power players carry more weight than others. When you hear one of these key people make a comment, it should attract special attention.

There are almost always characteristics that are not stated, but are still critical to success. These are usually less noble or desirable things. For this particular former employer, I could also add the following unstated, less desirable, but also highly valued characteristics: connections to important decision-makers outside the company, dedication as measured by hours worked and personal sacrifices made, going along to get along, and a willingness to communicate bad news immediately. Fall short on any of these, and you would be downgraded, or perhaps shown the door.

The art of managing your image within the organization mainly becomes a task of managing it along the dimensions you've identified as valued by the company. Do this well, and you're building on a solid foundation. When you get in the inevitable political battle, you will have the advantage of being perceived as a valuable asset who fits in. Do it poorly, and you're setting yourself up for difficulties.

How do you figure out what the valued dimensions are? The primary strategy is to watch and listen. What are other employees criticized for? If you hear constant complaints about clock-watching, or how quickly the parking lot clears out at 5:00 PM, or how irritating a late arriver is – you can surmise that time committed to work is an important dimension along which you will be judged.

Should you hear people criticized for emotional or angry outbursts, then "going along" may be highly valued. In one organization where I worked, people were criticized for *not* displaying over-the-top emotions – specifically anger – when challenged. It is essential that you take note of such things to understand the *real* values of the company.

Once you are aware of the behaviors and characteristics that are valued, it becomes your job to conform as best you can, and to manage others' perceptions of your conformance. Will you be the first one to the office in the morning and the last to leave at night? In an organization that values the hours you commit, that would be a good strategy. If you're willing to make the required sacrifices, they can only help you.

Chapter 14 – Be Careful What you Put in Writing

We've all seen it before – that horrible email sent by a foolish peer. You know the one. The inappropriate language. The insensitive and uncalled for comments. It's enough to boggle the mind. And we all know what happens to those emails – they end up circulated to anyone and everyone who might find the behavior offensive.

But if we've all seen it and know the result, why does it keep happening? I believe these incidents occur at the intersection of two not-so-unusual events – a political avoider or neutral who's in over his/her head, and a highly emotional situation in which this person feels a self-righteous urge to vent.

I used to ask my subordinates routinely, particularly those who were an important part of my team, to send me a preview of their emotional email before they actually pressed "send." This seemed to keep a lid on the worst of the behavior.

Email was where I first started seeing this kind of stuff, but today it's hardly limited to the company email account. Now you're at risk with anything you might post on your blog, Facebook account, Twitter, leave in a voicemail message (which can easily become digitized files that can be exchanged electronically), or deposit any other place where it's easy to copy and circulate.

So what's the secret to managing your writings to avoid ever being caught in this trap? How do you make sure you don't undermine yourself by giving your enemies plenty of ammunition to attack you?

First, warning bells should sound anytime you are typing and are simultaneously angry. If you can't stop, then please, please, please save whatever it is as a **draft** and hold off hitting "send." Initially address the email to yourself, to avoid a "fat finger" error of epic proportions. Once you've cooled off, re-read what you've written.

In most cases, at this point you'll delete it.

If you feel compelled to send it, first imagine your words on the front of the newspaper, in your church bulletin, or in the company newsletter. Would this kind of recognition make you proud? If not – delete.

If you still need to tell someone off – do it verbally, preferably when no one else is around to hear. Preferably away from the premises where the chances a co-worker will overhear the exchange are at least reduced. At the least a verbal response leaves some uncertainty in the minds of others as to exactly what happened. When it is put in writing, you've got nowhere to hide, but plenty of opportunity for misinterpretation.

Second, remember that anything you post on Facebook, Twitter, LinkedIn, or any other social media site is in the public domain. If juicy enough, or if discovered by an enemy, you can expect it to be used against you. If you must post insults about your employer, or naked pictures, or whatever, do so anonymously – and make damned sure it stays that way.

I've never personally seen someone (virtually) strung up for a social media post before, but did witness a manager lose considerable standing when a digitized voicemail of a rant was circulated to most of the senior management team in the office.

Being careful about what you put in writing is all about showing self-restraint and practicing emotional control. If you can't do that, you have no business playing the game of politics.

Chapter 15 – Lend Support Before you Need It

How do you build your political alliances and move your projects and ambitions forward? With the help of others – your allies. In order to have and maintain allies, it helps to have a positive balance with them in your political checking account. This "neutral" tactic is all about making sure you'll have support when you need it – when it really counts.

Can you build alliances without lending support to others? Sure. But *mutual* support is the glue that holds alliances together. Without sticking your neck out a little bit for others, they're not likely to stick their necks out for you.

How do you do this effectively?

Generally you should assume you will need to "give" before you "get." You need to demonstrate your commitment to other people and their agendas before you need their aid. Will you get burned by doing this? Sometimes – the tactic is not without some risk. There are power players out there (especially street fighters) who will gladly throw you under the bus if a situation where it is to their clear advantage to do so presents itself. Regardless of how much you've supported them in the past (memo to self: don't waste a lot of effort lending support to a street fighter). Be at peace with the fact you will probably give more than you get. You want that. That way you always keep a positive balance in your accounts.

I used to make a point of spending some time with each new peer that entered the organization – because I liked to meet new people, and also because I was subtly recruiting them to my "team." The conversations tended to focus on them – what they liked, what they thought about key issues, what ticked them off. My side of the discussion consisted of offering some free advice about the organization and what might get them in trouble – I was "giving" something inexpensive to me, but of value to the new guy. And while this technique didn't always produce a new political ally, it cost me almost nothing.

If you don't start by lending support, then you consign yourself to the virtual sidelines. Then you only play in the game when forced to do so, and most likely without a team behind you.

Build most of your alliances with other neutrals. By doing so, you are eschewing the more dangerous and distasteful tactics used by power players. As a neutral, you will make yourself an easy mark if you're too closely allied with these creatures – doing so makes you a prime target for *their* enemies. Working primarily with neutrals, you can count on things like friendship, a sense of obligation, and a belief in fair play to help you rally their support. Those things may not matter to a power player.

Lend mostly moral support. This can be in the form of a shoulder to cry on, a quiet counselor, a behind-the-scenes cheerleader. This costs you very little, and will pay dividends in the long term. I'm tempted to advise you to agree with everything your allies say and do – at least behind closed doors. But most neutrals will still feel a moral obligation to be honest. So instead, agree with as much as you can, and skimp on the criticism.

Just as with many of the other tactics, pick your battles carefully. You will find there are times when you need to lend public support to your allies. Do so sparingly, causing as little offense as possible, and making sure you know the impact of your actions. Most (but not all) people can accept a position taken against them, if it is taken on principle. Make sure the underlying rationale for your action is sound.

Occasionally, lend support to those you've opposed in the past. Opponents in a minor skirmish don't have to become long-term enemies. There is no better way to convert a former opponent into an ally than supporting them on something they find important. I was once able to recover a relationship after a particularly nasty public confrontation by extending several olive branches to the manager in the form of support for a project he was trying to get approved.

Master this tactic, and when you find yourself in a political jam, you'll have plenty of friends to help you. Ignore it at your own peril.

Chapter 16 – Make Sure Risks are Tilted in Your Favor

Risks are a part of corporate life, but all risks are not created equal. Some are…well…riskier. As an adept neutral, you need to be selective in the risks you are willing to accept and careful how you manage them. Generally, sticking with lower-risk projects and goals is the way to go, but don't be too conservative. If you successfully fend off all risks you won't have significant wins to show when senior management is tallying up its list of high-potential employees.

If you're climbing the corporate ladder, you're not going to move very far without the credit for some big accomplishments. Taking on those projects that produce big accomplishments can't be done without simultaneously accepting a measure of risk. Early in a career, the "promise of greatness" is enough to provide some momentum up the ladder. By mid-career, however, people begin to judge you on your track record – hopefully one that's impressive. You won't have much of a track record though if you won't take some risks.

Risks can be classified into four categories: "foolish" (low probability of success, low impact), "big gamble" (low probability of success, high impact), "sure thing" (high probability of success, high impact), and "inconsequential" (high probability of success, low impact). I suggest, if you want to survive and thrive, you look very hard for "sure things," and studiously avoid "big gambles." You shouldn't waste your time with either of the other two categories, because in the corporate world, a series of low impact wins does not total to a win with high impact. All those projects can do for your career is to present opportunities to be tagged with failures.

Alas, this was an area where I wasn't too good at following my own advice. I've always loved "big gamble" projects – ones with a medium-to-high risk and a huge payoff if it was a success. I used to try to have enough "irons in the fire" that I was pretty sure of having an ongoing string of big wins, ones that would allow people to ignore any failures. I lost a good position once, however, because I got the formula slightly out of balance, having a hiring failure, an acquisition failure, and a new production process failure all in succession. Had any one of them been a win, I probably would have been saved. Instead, the failed projects gave a power-playing competitor the opening he needed to get me fired. In hindsight, my entire strategy on personal risk management was flawed – I didn't need to take on all those risky projects. One or two "sure things" would have been much more helpful to my career. Lesson learned: take on too much risk, and eventually things will fall the wrong way, opening you up to political attack.

The capacity for, or even enjoyment of, taking risks (your personal or the company's "risk profile") varies considerably from person to person and organization to organization.

Companies that fire employees for failed projects (often having the feel of "punishment") are risk-averse. Companies that can accept failures as "learning opportunities" are more risk-tolerant. Watch what actually happens, and ignore what the CEO says on this subject – companies often seem to be either intentionally misleading or painfully unaware of where they fall on the risk-aversion scale. You need to get your risk-taking behavior in sync with the company's capacity and tolerance for risks. In most cases, the mismatch in risk profiles will be a personal risk capacity which is much higher than the organization's willingness to tolerate it, although the opposite does occasionally occur.

At one end of the personal risk profile spectrum are the ultra-conservatives – employees who avoid risk taking under any circumstances. They might only be provoked into accepting one risky project or goal per year, or even less if they can get away with it. Their biggest problem is that without a higher degree of risk taking, they aren't likely to build much of a track record of big accomplishments.

At the other extreme are gamblers – employees who agree to high targets, put a lot of balls in the air, and hope they will catch a few important ones. Generally, they're betting that when all successes and failures are tallied, they'll be judged a "keeper", and rewarded. Their biggest problem comes when too many things go south all at once. That's when they'll end up losing their job.

The craftiest way to have your cake and eat it too is to behave conservatively personally, but recruit a team of gamblers to work for you. You can sacrifice some of those gamblers when things go wrong by using a power player tactic known as scapegoating. If you're going to remain a neutral, however, this kind of political tactic is probably not something you can or want to use. Instead, you will have to position yourself carefully along the risk spectrum in order to succeed.

When in doubt, it is better to err on the conservative side of the risk-taking continuum. Why? The majority of companies seem to be fairly risk-averse, punishing people for taking chances and failing. In such environments, gamblers rarely seem to have much longevity. Eventually too many risks blow up on them simultaneously, and they flame out – exactly what happened to me.

Of course, you can be too conservative as well, being so afraid to try anything that you just muddle along with very few meaningful successes to your credit. People with this profile often last in their jobs, but rarely progress in their careers.

Chapter 17 – Presentations Count

How often do you get the opportunity to "strut your stuff" in front of the top people in the company? If you work for a large corporation, I'm guessing the answer is, "not often." And when you do get some "air time," it's probably in the form of some kind of presentation.

Senior managers are the ones who can make things happen for you. They can think of you when that next juicy project comes along, or that next promotion, or when it's time for raises. It doesn't take a lot of insight to recognize those few contacts with the senior people are pretty darned important.

What you may not realize, however, is *how* these senior managers form their opinions about you – at least if you're one of the people they don't work with on a daily basis. So here's the secret – it's 20% based on what's in your performance review, 30% based on what others are saying about you, and 50% based on direct observations. Maybe the numbers aren't really that precise, but you get the idea – your performance when presenting to those key decision-makers is critical.

I had a boss who would decide an employee was either a genius or an idiot within five minutes of them opening their mouths during a presentation. And once that employee fell into the "idiot" category, there was virtually no redeeming him/her. We can argue about the fairness of his judgments, but like many aspects of corporate life, *fair* or *unfair* has little bearing on the situation. He made his judgments based on an employee's ability to communicate ideas in a clear, concise fashion, to speak intelligently, and to respond to questions well. Are those the critical characteristics separating performers from non-performers? No, of course not. But his judgments did still stunt many a career, justified or not.

To a greater or lesser degree, pretty much all senior executives do the same thing. I can't tell you the number of times I've heard someone remark "she's smart," after a particularly good presentation, or "he's in over his head" (or something much less kind) after a bad one. Do those senior execs really know their conclusions are correct? No. They extrapolate based on a short snippet of data they gather during a presentation.

The judgments can easily become self-fulfilling prophesies, particularly the harsher ones. Senior managers sometimes act like sharks who smell blood in the water, and then launch into a feeding frenzy. The "idiot" is picked apart over every tiny misstep, while the "genius" is forgiven his errors based on a faith in his overall brilliance.

So what do you do in the face of this political reality? The path to success is no great secret: your presentations must be of the highest quality, and they need to wow the audience. To get that to happen, follow these simple steps:

1. Master the subject you are going to present. Make sure your depth of knowledge on the subject

equals or exceeds the most knowledgeable person in the audience. Cram if you have to. Understand the underlying theory informing the subject matter, too. Not just the way it is handled in your organization.

2. Get your slides and words right! Nobody is impressed by poor grammar, uneducated phrasing, misspellings, or other careless mistakes. Often, senior executives have slide pet peeves. Ask around to figure out what those are. I personally disliked the use of 3D graphs, for instance. I've known other executives to abhor reading off the slides during the presentation, or even the injudicious use of the color red. Getting your slides perfect is tough to do on your own – get some help, either from professionals, allies, or both. Even after years of making board presentations, it took one of my peers to point out to me the frequency with which I used the word "obviously."

3. There are bonus points for introducing fresh or innovative ways of looking at things. These may come from theory, experiences from other firms, or even directly out of your imagination. They affirm your mastery of the subject and get the audience thinking in new ways. It isn't necessary to overdo it, however. One new idea per presentation is plenty.

Presentations are a big deal, and they deserve a big application of your time and effort. You can miss a lot of smaller stuff in your job, but as long as you get these big events right, your political position will be strengthened.

Chapter 18 – Don't Hide Bad News

Some things get better with age. Bad news, however, is never one of them. Generally, bad news ferments and gets progressively smellier and uglier as time passes. It is best to get rid of it as soon as possible.

Tossing bad news out on the table at the wrong time, or in the wrong way will likely lead to more problems rather than fewer, and possibly a lot of "help" you don't want or need. How should you handle the revelation? Here are some tips to make bad news a bit more palatable.

1. Err on the side of mentioning potential problems before they become big, hairy monsters. If you're worried that the date might slip on that project – say you're worried now, rather than when everybody already knows about it. If you wait, people think you're either out of the loop or purposely hiding things.

2. Always think through the answer to one important question before you mention bad (or potentially bad) news – "What are you going to do about it?" You should be prepared to provide the answer to this question without prompting. Remember the

often quoted definition of insanity: continuing to do the same thing, but expecting different results. Tell management what you're going to do differently moving forward.

3. Package your bad news in a "bad news sandwich." Do this by taking the two best pieces of news you have and placing them before and immediately after your bad news. Sure, it won't nullify the bad, but at least it leaves the impression that everything isn't going down the tubes all at once. I've successfully used this technique many times, and it is always a lot better than just flopping out the problem all by itself.

4. Don't make people drag bad news out of you – volunteer it up front. Senior management will quickly conclude you can't be trusted if you repeatedly make them dig for problems. Show that you are perceptive enough to recognize what's important and what's not going right.

5. Don't pile on. Don't reveal your bad news as just one more problem in a seemingly endless series of issues (yours or those belonging to others). You don't want your bit of bad news to be the one that "breaks the camel's back." That can have deep and unpredictable repercussions. If others appear to be disgorging lots of bad news, hold on to yours for another time.

The bottom line is, bad news is just what it is...bad. There's a limited amount you can do to package it prettily, or to deflect the damage it causes.

Power players have some additional options when it comes to really bad news – tactics like distancing themselves from the failure and inserting scapegoats. By using scapegoats, power players don't reduce the impact of bad news, they simply deflect it onto someone else. Skilled scapegoaters will set things up well in advance, always keeping a buffer between themselves and their risks. This tactic is described in more detail in Chapter 29. Short of utilizing power-player tactics, however, the best thing you can do as a neutral is to limit the risks you take so that a minimal amount of bad news comes your way.

One thing you absolutely, positively should never, ever do, however, is hold off revealing bad news in the hope that something (e.g., a miracle) will occur to make it all work out. I remember a particular engineering manager who did this on a new production process he was responsible for developing. He eventually backed himself into such a terrible corner when his "miracle" solution didn't work that he was forced to resign without the hope of a positive reference from anyone in the company. If you start heading down this path, it's highly likely you, too, won't pull your head out of the sand until you have a huge, unrecoverable mess on your hands. Playing this game is a good way to get fired.

Chapter 19 – Don't Badmouth Your Enemies

It's a known fact that misery loves company, so how could something that feels as natural and comfortable as complaining about, criticizing, or otherwise badmouthing an enemy be the wrong thing to do?

There are two good reasons to avoid badmouthing: first, whatever you *think* you're saying in confidence to a friend or trusted associate is likely to get back to the object of your complaining. You should just assume it is going to happen and act accordingly. Second, since political alliances tend to shift continuously, today's enemy or competitor may be tomorrow's friend (or vice versa) – that is, unless your badmouthing has permanently poisoned the relationship.

In several chapters of this book, I've tried to show the fluidity of the political environment. Alliances change all the time. People receive new jobs, are assigned new responsibilities, set new goals, and aspire to, acquire or develop new ambitions. Projects fail, projects succeed, and the company moves forward. But harsh, personalized criticism lives on forever. That irritating power player – the one who made you extremely angry when he tried to scapegoat you on his bombing project – might be your best friend tomorrow when you need someone to help negate a rival's political clout. He might be an ally, unless he found out you labeled him a weasel and took it personally.

Remember the old chestnut, *this isn't personal, it's just business,* and try to take it to heart. If you feel compelled to criticize, then do so with someone who doesn't have a connection to your employer, like your pet Golden Retriever.

Why do these criticisms end up coming back to the object of your dissatisfaction like iron filings to a magnet? Because they represent valuable political currency that someone is likely to trade on. And don't think doing your badmouthing to a political avoider is the answer, either. They might pass it along because it's interesting, and they probably won't understand the value or potential damage inherent in the information.

I had a peer while working in one of my jobs who couldn't seem to resist the urge to run down other executives. Over time, he managed to offer harsh criticisms for almost everyone on the senior staff. The problem was, he didn't realize many of these comments were making it back to the people he talked about – a quid pro quo exchange. Eventually, he alienated all his peers, and when he needed support during a particularly nasty public interrogation and flogging over the poor performance of one of his acquisitions, no one was interested in coming to his aid. In fact, we all smugly felt he deserved it.

If, for some reason, you mistakenly or uncontrollably badmouth someone against my advice, at least have the sense to avoid loaded terms like: liar, cheat, scumbag, weasel, and similar labels. Those words are meant to brand someone's entire character, and they are almost impossible to retract.

And if you do even that, then start assessing what the damage might be when the target of your badmouthing hears what you've said (no doubt embellished by those in the "telephone game" gossip path). You may choose to live with the damage, or you may decide you need to go bow and scrape before the person to try to negate it – your choice, but at least be aware of and be willing to accept the potential consequences.

Asking for forgiveness is a powerful remedy, but you can't count on it to work universally. One of my managers once referred to one of his peers in a different division as a "self-serving jerk" (justified, in my opinion) behind his back, and when the label reached this particular executive's ears, he couldn't be pacified despite a seemingly ridiculous amount of apologizing. My manager created an enemy that plagued him for the rest of his time at the company (which was blissfully short).

Chapter 20 – Keep Complaints to Yourself

What do most people do when they're unhappy?

They share – their feelings, their frustrations, and their anger.

In most cases they're looking for commiseration and sympathy.

But is seeking commiseration from your fellow workers a wise or a foolish move? The answer without a doubt is foolish, and there are two big reasons.

Everything you say to anyone in the work environment – even your most trusted allies – can and often does become political ammunition. I've seen this happen far too many times, and if you're politically attuned, you probably have as well. To see this kind of ammo being used, just look for a comment prefaced by, "Bill thinks..." or "Jane is really angry about...." In all likelihood, the person mentioned in the statement is, at that very moment, being betrayed by the speaker. The reason may be as insignificant as for a laugh, or as weighty as to change the power alignment in an important debate. Whatever the reason for the betrayal, it couldn't have happened if the original confessor had simply kept their unhappiness to themselves.

A second reason to keep your unhappiness hidden has been made much more obvious by a recent corporate focus on "engaged" versus "disengaged" employees. Empirical evidence shows that "engaged" employees (however they might be defined) are much more productive than "disengaged" employees. Duh! And there are two classes of the disengaged – active and inactive. By complaining to a fellow employee, you not only potentially boot yourself out of the ranks of the "engaged" employees, you risk being labeled as "actively disengaged," the most damning classification possible.

Unfortunately, the conventional solution to having "actively disengaged" employees is to get them out of the company. No planned rehabilitation, just fire 'em. The only way to ensure you aren't classified as "actively disengaged" is not to *look* "actively disengaged" (and be extremely careful what you say on any employee opinion survey, especially if there's any chance of identifying individual survey results).

So what's an employee to do? If you're stuck with that micro-manager as a boss (or whatever your personal cross is to bear), somehow you must learn to suffer through it. Silently.

If you must talk it out – do so only with someone outside the company. Or better yet, tell it to your dog.

If you want to offer constructive criticism, then go beyond just complaining, offer real alternatives and suggest a way to make improvements. Then get involved in making it happen. Under those circumstances, you should talk to the person who is the focus of your issue, not a pal in the office (or plant). Critique is understood by senior managers as being less than one percent of what is needed to improve the organization. Employees that get involved in implementing improvements are appreciated. Whiners are not.

Section 4 – Tactics for Power Players

Chapter 21 – Actively Manage Your Reputation

Now we move from the realm of the political neutral into that of the power player. While many of the techniques I discuss here are applicable to both *maneuverers* and *street fighters*, I will be presenting them from the perspective of the maneuverer.

Reputation is critically important to your political success in any large organization, and being aware of and managing that reputation is one of the things all power players must do well.

So how do you go about accomplishing this?

The first step is to be aware of where you currently stand. In most cases, peers and subordinates are quick to tell you about your strengths, but are hesitant to point out areas of perceived weakness. It is in these areas of weakness, however, where your greatest vulnerabilities lie. No matter how uncomfortable it might make you, you must discover the weak spots in your current reputation.

The best way to do this is with the help of carefully selected confidants. Whether mentors, peers, or implicitly trusted subordinates, these people can collect information to which you will never have access and feed it back to you.

No doubt, mentors and/or confidants will be some of your most valuable relationships in the political corporation.

In one of my jobs where I reported to the CEO, understanding where you stood was nearly impossible – at least if you were depending on your own observations. He was intentionally vague, and sometimes outright deceptive, when dealing with subordinates. My job was saved on more than one occasion by whispers collected by friends on the corporate staff. Without that input, I would have hopelessly flailed about trying to figure out what weak point was vulnerable at any particular time.

In most organizations it is important to be seen as smart, hardworking, and an innovative thinker. If you are coming up short on any of these dimensions, quick action is needed to rescue your reputation.

And how does one *fix* a deficient reputation? By remembering that perception is reality. Your first line of defense is your own track record. If you are challenged on your creativity, make sure to trumpet the latest new idea you've had that (hopefully) benefited the company. If you don't have your own idea, perhaps you've at least associated yourself with someone else's. If your work ethic is the problem, emphasize the sacrifices you've made in the past for the betterment of the company. Make sure these stories are repeated to anyone and everyone with political influence – better if it is someone other than you tooting your horn, as tooting your own is sometimes viewed as distasteful.

Think about ways you can build your reputation – ones that offset any weakness which is now vulnerable. It's always been amazing to me that the person who generates useless ideas is often valued more highly than the one that delivers results, but that is the way things sometimes work. Make sure to suggest new, innovative, and clever concepts, even if they go nowhere. Often, those concepts can be drawn from popular business publications – just make sure you're on the leading edge of the idea at your company, as opposed to a late convert. And make sure *no one* can criticize your work ethic – be the first in the office and the last to leave more often than not.

Beyond smart, hardworking, and innovative, let your company's values be your guide. If you're truly a power player, you already know the behaviors that are valued by the company. To succeed, you must assess and manage your reputation along all of these dimensions.

Perception is reality. In the political environment, one of your chief tasks is to manage those perceptions. Reputation is the measuring stick, so always be aware of how what you do might impact it.

Chapter 22 – Cultivate a Mentor

I listed mentors under the power player tactics, even though many neutrals can benefit from a mentor. too. I do this because only an aspiring power player can take fullest advantage of a mentoring relationship.

There are four primary reasons why you should cultivate a mentor:

1. A mentor is usually more senior in the organization and generally already knows the lay of the land. Having access to a mentor immediately helps you better understand such things as organization values and the existing informal power structure.

2. Mentors can teach you the skills in their toolboxes that you don't yet possess. If your mentor is an expert scapegoater, for instance, she can tell (and show) you how to use the tactic. If she is particularly good at setting credibly low goals and targets, you learn the tactic faster with active help from your mentor. Of course, you can learn all the tactics on your own – through a combination of observation and trial and error, but having a

journey(wo)man-mentor available to counsel you makes the process faster and less risky.

3. Mentors will normally take your side. When you're searching for allies to push through approval on that controversial project, your mentor should be at the front of the line rallying help. And she might even tip you off that you're beating a dead horse, if you need to drop the effort altogether before doing some serious damage to your reputation.

4. Mentors *can be* confidants. Remember when I discussed "keeping it to yourself," I said if you need someone to whine to about work – get a dog? Well, the only possible exception to that rule would be your mentor, and even then only after the relationship has had a good period of time to mature. Mentors generally will never throw their mentee under the bus. But if your mentor is an expert blame-deflector or scapegoater, better to be cautious in this area. When it comes down to either him or you, consistent with his power-player nature, he's going to make sure it's you.

Picking a mentor can be tricky. While it's easy to outline the desirable characteristics, there is an element of good fortune involved in finding the right relationship.

On paper, the ideal mentor is: high up in the organization, politically adept in the same style you've chosen for yourself (a maneuverer for budding maneuverers, a street fighter for aspiring street fighters), and a long-term company survivor – you don't want to develop your mentor relationship only to have the mentor jump ship for an opportunity at a different company. The tricky part is the need for some personal chemistry.

Normally, there is mutual respect between the two people in the relationship, and normally the mentor sees underdeveloped potential in the mentee. You can work at making yourself appealing along this dimension, but doing so still doesn't ensure good chemistry – which seems to come more from similar points of view and/or shared experiences. Making the chemistry work is something you'll need to figure out for yourself.

Do CEO's mentor? I've been asked this question a number of times. Not surprisingly, most rising power players would love to reach for the stars, hoping to land the big boss as their mentor. I've never personally witnessed a CEO mentoring, but I'm sure there must be examples of it out there somewhere. At the least, the nature of a CEO's job responsibilities – things like managing succession plans for the company, or the need to appear impartial – make acting as a mentor a bit trickier. The CEO's that I've known would never open themselves up to the degree other executives are often willing to do. Despite the lure, I'd advise you to set your sights a little lower than the CEO when shopping for a mentor.

In choosing my personal mentor, I violated a few of my basic rules of thumb I just laid out. While he was several levels higher in the organization than I was, he was a relative newcomer. But the essential chemistry was present from the early going. It developed because of my willingness to be open about how things worked at the company (which was of value to him) and our shared interests in books and film. And I was eager to drink up every drop of advice and every observation about business he was willing to offer. The point is, finding a mentor is not like shopping for a used car, where you want to get the absolute best one – there is a bit of serendipity in the entire process.

My mentor was also my direct supervisor, at least on two occasions, which I normally wouldn't recommend. It worked in this case because he was my mentor before he was my boss. Mentor-mentee relationships tend to transcend the normal reporting structure. If you have a subordinate, peer, or enemy with a mentor aiding them, you want to be well aware of it – my mentor protected me from ambitious competitors more than once, with disastrous results for my opponent.

Some senior managers become mentors because they have a strong need/desire to help younger employees starting early in their careers. They are the exception rather than the rule. Other senior managers seem to migrate to the mentoring role as they reach and pass the apex of their careers. I believe this phenomenon is a "coming to grips" with the approaching end of their corporate battles. Perhaps they see the next generation of corporate leadership taking shape and want to help favored candidates. Whatever the reason, those near their career summits do seem to make better targets for the rising power player to approach.

Chapter 23 – Ask for What You Want

Ambition is a two-edged sword – express it, letting people know you've set your career sights higher, and you'll capture people's attention – both good and bad. By expressing your ambitions you're letting people know that you believe you have more to offer, and perhaps inadvertently communicating you are a force to be reckoned with.

Of course, you could express no ambition – in which case you will likely be judged as dull, complacent, or satisfied with your current lot in life. That might be fine if you have no desire to climb further up the corporate ladder – perhaps even a plus, as it partially neutralizes the tendency for other power players to see you as a threat. If you are good – really good – someone will eventually ask why you aren't aiming higher. You likely won't be able to hide your abilities forever.

For a ladder-climber, expressing ambition is critical to long-term success. If people are unaware that you are "a player," they are much less likely to take you seriously. And the likelihood of moving into the roles and jobs in which you're interested is quite low if you're depending solely on luck to get you there.

So what's the best way to ask for what you want? This is a subject where discussing both "do's" and "don'ts" provides clearer insight.

1. Don't be impatient. I had a manager approach me just a few days after I joined one of my employers – he wanted to know what he needed to do to "get ahead" at the company. The discussion felt so odd and forced, I couldn't help but think he was strange. Be keenly aware there is a time and place to express your ambitions to others – the best time being after a rousing success.

2. Don't criticize someone in your target position, and then follow up with commentary about how much better *you'd* be doing the job. Even if your audience agrees with the criticism (which won't earn you any points), they will likely find your brazen undermining distasteful. I'll grant a possible exception to this advice for extremely skilled street fighters – but pulling it off requires exceptional finesse. One of my bosses, a street fighter, was particularly good at executing this tactic. I can't recommend such an approach for the vast majority of people.

3. Don't be too specific, or too short-term. Don't say you want "Fred's job" – there's no more certain way to make an enemy of Fred when he finds out. A better approach is to take aim at a position two or three levels above you. "I'd love to be a plant manager some day" is a much safer approach, and it communicates the ambition just as effectively. There is a time to ask for Fred's job – when it

106

becomes known he's leaving it. Then you shouldn't hesitate to make your interest plain.

4. Keep quiet if your recent performance level hasn't quite been up to snuff. A highly ambitious and demanding employee who is underperforming is likely to earn a quick ticket out of the game entirely.

5. Do make visible efforts to improve yourself. A night MBA isn't the only way to do it – reading, demonstrating new skills and proficiencies, or attending seminars or conferences can also help. As a rule of thumb, I'd recommend making at least one visible effort to improve your skills each year. If you set your sights on an additional degree (like an MBA) you may have to change companies to achieve improvements in your position. Companies, much like the homelands of biblical prophets, seem to have a tough time thinking of their newly degreed employees differently than they did when the employee first started with the organization.

6. Before you say anything to anybody, recognize what you're signing up for when you express ambition – you may not know when and from where the next opportunity will come. It may require a physical move, a change in departments, or working for a current political enemy. It may happen when your kid is in her senior year of high school. Don't start the clock ticking if you're likely to refuse. Refusals can typically only be made once in a great while. Otherwise the senior management team will decide you really aren't a serious candidate.

Can you be a great politician without expressing ambition? You bet. Not all great politicians are engaged in climbing the corporate ladder. But by indicating your desire to advance your career, you put yourself into the stream of political power players.

Chapter 24 – Set the Bar Credibly Low

Most of us would agree superior performance is critical to an individual's success in most organizations. The problem comes when we try to measure it. It's easy to kid ourselves into believing numerical targets are the most objective way to measure people, but what is often forgotten is that these measurements always have to be compared to some sort of standard. The standards themselves are filled with biases, poor assumptions, and bad estimates. If standards were re-evaluated at the end of the performance period, many wouldn't legitimately be usable to make pronouncements about the individual being evaluated. Priorities change, initial forecasts prove to be incorrect, markets behave in unexpected ways. Yet corporations still cling to their numerical targets, as if *wishing* they were correct is all that matters. The prudent power player acknowledges this situation by making certain their personal targets are set at a level as low as is credibly possible.

If a company saw a five percent drop in earnings in a year, most people would call that a failure – unless the year was 2009, when the vast majority of companies saw declines of twenty percent or more. And when the goals passed down by corporate CEO's were set in stone in late 2008, do you think many foresaw such a steep drop in earnings? Most of them probably imposed targets to drive increased earnings for that disastrous year, which their organizations then went on to miss miserably. Was a five percent decline really a failure?

It depends on what you measure it against.

This may seem obvious, but let me make sure to be clear about it – there is no upside to allowing your personal performance targets to be set high. It is in your best interest to make sure your targets are set as low as possible. Impossibly high targets set you up for a series of disappointments that leave your corporate superiors with a bad taste in the mouths. Even goals that look reasonable at the time can wreck you when something unexpected happens. By setting your personal bar lower, you should have a cushion to help absorb some of those unexpected events.

Start by exploring, with as much discipline as possible, all the things that can go wrong in the coming performance period (usually, a year). Focus particularly on those items outside of your control such as: the economy, interest rates, your customers' sales and their financial well-being, possible competitive strategies, etc. Take a credibly pessimistic view on each one of these as you negotiate your targets.

By "credibly pessimistic," I mean a forecast or scenario that is still in the mainstream, but below the median. As an example, the potential for a "double dip" recession should have been built into 2010's goals. Sure, it didn't actually happen, but there was plenty of uncertainty surrounding the subject. In 2012, the big economic bogeyman was

Greek/Spanish/Portugese/Italian economic viability and the future of the Euro. These pessimistic situations should loom large in your overall target setting.

"But won't I look like a naysayer? Won't I seem hopelessly pessimist?" you may ask.

No, because you must also show confidence in your performance on the factors you do control – your new product, a new pricing program, that cost reduction. Now, don't go crazy here – you still want the overall target to be "credibly" low. The desired effect is a fairly bleak external picture improved upon "some" by your efforts. Where "some" is as small an impact as you can convince people it has to be.

There is some craft required to sell this. And everyone has seen variations of it before, so they're likely to roll their eyes a bit. But the bottom line is, there just isn't any better way to approach the problem. If you let your targets be set based on median views of the future, then you'll "fail" at least half the time.

Another thing you must pay attention to is the accumulation of numerous small risks. If there is a small but real chance of three things independently going wrong, but if any one of them happens you will fail, then you've got a fairly big problem. Three small but real risks equals something greater than a small chance of failure – it equals a moderate chance. If there are four risks, the chances of failure go up further. Five is even worse. And so on....

For example, if you have responsibility for several P&Ls, projects, or cost reductions, make sure you don't just add up the expected results of all the individual pieces and make that your goal. Something will likely go wrong somewhere, and unless you build that probability into your targets you'll have an overall failure on your hands.

Finally, if you have subordinates, you must pass along a collective target to them that is higher than the one you are signing up for. Sometimes considerably higher. Someone responsible for carrying out a piece of the project (or P&L) will fail, and you need to have others striving for a higher number to offset the failure.

If this tactic seems unfair or slightly deceptive, remember it is in the province of the power player, where there are numerous elements of political playing that some might consider "unsavory." The prudent power player does everything within his or her ability to make sure to record wins – including fighting to set low targets, and covering their risks.

Chapter 25 – Provide Some Original Thinking

One of my most successful and influential bosses once told me he tried to introduce at least one new or innovative concept at every major presentation. That boss was respected for his intelligence and his creativity. You can be similarly respected, too, simply by following his advice.

The characteristics, talents, skills, and behaviors valued by organizations vary considerably from one company to another. One of my employers highly valued *going along to get along*, another promoted people who were confrontational, another valued people who were willing to put in long hours. There were probably greater differences between these three companies than there were similarities.

But they all shared one common value – they all wanted "smart" people to fill the critical roles of their organizations. I'm talking book-smart here – high IQ – not necessarily emotionally intelligent, which is an entirely different subject. Intelligence was valued in and for itself. It was as if senior management put blind faith in the idea that if you put a bunch of smart people together, the whole adds up to more than the sum of the parts.

In fact, I can't think of a single organization I've ever dealt with where being smart wasn't a get-out-of-jail-free card, at least to a degree.

Senior Manager number one: "He can't seem to get that project to work."

Senior Manager number two: "Yeah, but he's so smart – if he can't figure it out, it must be impossible."

Many of you have probably witnessed similar behavior.

To become known for your "smarts," there are two things you need to do: the first one hardly bears mentioning – don't do or say stupid things. It's not hard doing this most of the time, but doing it all the time can be quite challenging. Most of us have a slip now and again, and our peers and superiors judge us harshly when we either "don't get it" or misread a situation. I don't know how to advise you to avoid making dumb errors, other than telling you to take your time and make sure you know what you're saying before opening your mouth.

I once cringed while watching a subordinate give our CEO an impossibly high estimate for the number of potential customers in a distant Asian country. He'd tried to calculate the figure in his head, and had missed by a couple of orders of magnitude. The room broke into laughter when one of the other executives said, "I think he means the number of chickens, not customers." The situation would have been fine at that point, if the executive hadn't then tried to insist he was right. The guy was knocked down a couple of notches in perceived intelligence in the eyes of the CEO right then and there.

The second thing you need to do is bring some new ideas to the organization. When you present something new, you're seen as having a degree of expertise in the area in which you're introducing the idea – and you better have it in reality, so bone up on your subject matter before presenting anything. It might be a new way of looking at old data. It could be an improved method, or a cost-reduction project. Whatever it is, it should offer insight and opportunities that are new to your bosses.

Being judged as smart will come a little at a time – at first people may think you are simply a one-trick pony, but repeatedly coming up with new and innovative ideas will push you along the "smartness" path rapidly.

And now for a little secret – the ideas don't have to be world-altering. They don't have to be far-reaching in impact. In fact, they don't even need to be implemented or actually lead anywhere. It is the introduction of the new insight – one that produces that "ah-ha" moment – which makes all the difference.

Chapter 26 – Promote Yourself

"He who tooteth not his own horn, will not his horn have tooted."

A favorite saying from a prior boss, but definitely one with some truth behind it. If you want to gain attention for your accomplishments, you need to make others aware of them. The most miraculous business save, if accomplished without the knowledge of your peers and superiors, is wasted. Sure, you could sit around feeling angry, while reasoning that people *should* know, that it is *their job* to know, but that won't get you anywhere.

On the other hand, in all the corporate environments I've known, there is a fine line between subtle tooting and obnoxious self-promotion. Fall into the latter category, and you are likely to be scorned.

The bad news is, I don't know how to tell you where the line is between these two. It varies a bit by company, and also by what you're crowing over. I can, however, suggest the following procedure:

1. Be cautious, and watch others. Specifically watch for someone who is in the "obnoxious self-promoter" category. Observe specifically what

he/she is doing that crosses the line, and vow never, ever to do those things. Then identify someone who is doing a good job of tactful tooting, and note their behaviors that are effective in getting the point across without annoying others.

2. Talk about the magnitude of the success you've achieved, but make sure to compliment (primarily) the *others* who were involved. Take little or no credit yourself. Tell everyone how it wouldn't have been possible if Sally hadn't gotten you that price analysis, or how well Bob handled that angry call from the customer. It will get the point across about the accomplishment, and will at least have a hint of palatable humility.

3. Want to go one step further? Get Sally, Bob, or both to also tell the story, but in *their* version they give *you* the credit. Again, it accomplishes the tooting without the obnoxious aftertaste.

There are two ways to make the arrangement described above with your co-workers – first, you could overtly negotiate it with Sally. I must admit I've never tried this, as it always seemed a bit "unseemly." (My unwillingness, on this and other tactics, is the key reason I was never a highly successful power player.) If you are sure of your relationship with the person, and want to get the best advantage from the success, there isn't much that can beat a plainly spoken understanding.

The second method is the "bragging" version of *the virtuous circle*. Compliment Bob on his piece of the success when he's present, and then depend on him to return the favor. If Bob is at least a political neutral, he should catch on. Of course, if he's an avoider or a street fighter, this probably won't work. He'll either be puzzled by your actions, or try to turn the situation further to his advantage.

Remember, power players – especially maneuverers – need to draw positive attention to themselves, and self-promotion is one of the most effective ways to do that. Done effectively, it is unlikely to result in retaliation or ill will. Self-promotion is an important part of the power player's arsenal.

Chapter 27 – Distance Yourself from Failure

"Success has many fathers, but failure is an orphan."

That's the way most of us wish things worked, but that's not been my experience in large corporations. In fact, there seems to be a relentless drive to pin blame for anything remotely perceived as a failure on some poor, hapless employee/victim. Occasionally it's justified, but most often, not.

Forget about the unreasonable goals, often established in a vacuum by someone who wasn't going to have to deliver them. Never mind that the original strategy was fundamentally flawed. Don't even consider the unexpected and unpredictable circumstances that arose during implementation. There is a person, somewhere in the organization, who is responsible for this failure. Find him.

This seems to be the mantra in the corporate blame game. Every problem – every failure – has to have a name attached to it.

If you want to survive and thrive in the political world, you better make sure that name *isn't* yours.

And, as with many of the admonitions I've presented in this book, that point is probably obvious to experienced political players. You don't want to be nailed as the one who failed. The question really becomes – how?

Here are three ways to make sure it doesn't happen to you:

1. Don't sign up for a project with a high-risk of failure. Of course, sometimes it's hard to do this – your position may make it impossible to avoid a bad strategy being advanced by your boss, for example. But in many cases you have more control over signing up than you think.

2. Narrow the scope of your part of the project, and make sure you can claim success for that part – even if the rest ultimately fails. You can actually get a small amount of positive recognition for nicely rearranging the deck chairs on the company's Titanic, if you do it particularly well. If you own the entire project, however, this option isn't open to you.

3. Get on record early as having grave concerns about the project's success and your desire to avoid it. Doing so can at least make you look smart when the whole thing is going down the tubes. If by some miracle the project later succeeds, few will recall you were an early doubter. This, like many techniques, must be delivered with craft. Overplay your hand, and people may try to pin the "self-fulfilling prophesy" label on you, and shift even more of the blame in your direction. It can also backfire, and cause you to pick up more scope when you are trying to narrow your exposure.

Scapegoating can also be used in this situation – a tactic I will be turning to in Chapter 29. But scapegoating has a greater scope than just distancing oneself from a failure, so I will defer further discussion of that tactic until then.

Keeping failures off your record is critical to playing successfully in the higher-levels within corporations. Keeping them off also helps to avoid other power players taking advantage of you. Distance yourself from failure well, and you've mastered nearly all the tactics in the power player's handbook.

Chapter 28 – Expect Betrayal

Most business relationships are superficial. It may not feel that way all the time, but if you've ever changed companies, you can verify my assertion. How many of your old associates do you still spend time with? For most people, the answer is not very many. In your next job, you develop a collection of new superficial business relationships, and those, plus normal time demands, force out the old. After all, there are only so many hours in the day, right?

Real relationships are deeper than just the convenience of the moment. They are built on shared interests and experiences, true respect, and interdependence. Superficial business relationships tend to be based on proximity, and the needs of constantly shifting alliances.

Some business relationships do develop into real relationships. But it takes hard work to make it happen, and the relationship has to transcend the politics of the office. Most employees would willingly sacrifice an enemy/competitor, often would sacrifice a peer, but rarely would sacrifice a friend. Finding the critical few relationships that can grow into real friendships is very important to your power base – these are the relationships on which you can usually depend. True mentor relationships, for example, should certainly fall into this category.

I say "usually" because I've seen a handful of shocking betrayals in my days in executive leadership. While buying a small business, I watched as the majority owner was callously betrayed by his partner and supposed best friend. The betrayer was not happy with the changes the sale would mean, and rather than speaking up and having his issues addressed, he surreptitiously worked with our primary competitor, revealing critical details of the deal. When the acquisition happened anyway, he was set up by the competitor with a rival business in the same town as his former "best friend."

So watch your back.

And by "watching your back," I mean critically examining your friends' actions and behaviors for inconsistencies. In the biggest betrayals I've seen, hindsight showed there were signs, but the victims ignored them in favor of their faith in their ultimate betrayers.

For your other "everyday, run-of-the-mill" relationships, just remember these are like the alliances on the TV show *Survivor* – merrily made today, only to be dissolved tomorrow when the need arises. One aspect of *Survivor* that has continually fascinated me is the anger felt by so many of the contestants once they discover they've been thrown over for a better (or more expedient) coalition. Duh.

The same thing happens in the business world. Don't be surprised (or angry) when your friend-of-convenience today becomes your opposition tomorrow. It happens all the time – and it's not personal. It's just business.

Lastly, and I've cautioned this often within these pages, be very careful about the ammunition you put into the hands of others. Don't be lulled into revealing too much to allies. The information you share with them is exactly what they will use should they switch sides – and what will get you into trouble.

Chapter 29 – Invest in Scapegoats

Now we come to what is considered by some to be the most abhorrent of all political tactics – scapegoating. This is a maneuverer's tactic, much more so than a street fighter's. Street fighters use the force of their personalities in their political battles, where maneuverers are more subtle. All of the "master maneuverers" I personally know are also masters of scapegoating.

Scapegoating is the transference of blame for a business failure (project, financial performance, bad hire, etc.) from one person's shoulders onto those of another. In most instances where I've seen this happen, the business failure had its roots in a flawed strategy or bad assumptions, and the architect of the whole thing positions some other poor sap to take the fall, blaming the failure on poor implementation.

"When a problem develops, you dive down. I go up."

This advice was perhaps the closest I ever came to understanding what happens inside the head of the maneuverer when he or she plays this card. This meant that when a problem arose in a project or business unit, I tended to dig into the details personally, while the speaker made sure to insert someone between himself and the problem. Looking at it from a moralistic viewpoint, scapegoating appears to be a shameless shucking of blame, allowing the fallout to settle on the shoulders of innocents. I could never do it – not because I didn't understand the technique, but simply because it seemed so…wrong.

You may have a different sense of right and wrong. Or maybe certain circumstances make the act of scapegoating less repugnant. For whatever reason, if you're going to do it, you should employ the tactic wisely and correctly.

There are two keys to successful scapegoating – timing and proper selection of the "goat."

From a timing standpoint, the earlier in a project that you are able to lay the groundwork, the better. I'd advise you to start planning a scapegoat as a back-up plan for any high-risk project. I'd certainly recommend you put the scapegoat in place as soon as you see the first indications of trouble.

What do I mean by "put in place"? Specifically maneuver the scapegoat into a position where that person is responsible for the thing at risk – the critical part of the project, or the whole thing. Make them the project manager, or a specialist focusing on the "at risk" area, if it is a project. Make them the sponsoring manager, if it is an acquisition.

You're certainly giving up the opportunity to take the lion's share of the credit for success (in the unlikely event the project is miraculously converted into a win). If the project succeeds, however, you will still share in the glory, perhaps just not taking center stage. If the project fails, you will have distanced yourself sufficiently so as not to have too much blame cast your way. It's an insurance policy –

take it out when you develop a sniffle, not when you're on life support. By then it costs too much, and the patient is likely to die anyway.

Selecting the right scapegoat can be an art in itself. In most cases, a requirement for success is for the "goat" to be your own subordinate, and for them to be acknowledged in the organization as a "good performer," and a "good fit" for the role.

Anyone else is likely to cast all blame for any failing back toward you if the project goes down the tubes. Blame-shedding could still happen with a subordinate, but it's less likely, particularly if you put them in place *blindly*. By that, I mean the goat doesn't realize why he/she is actually there – as a buffer between you and potential failure. You achieve this by stroking their ego and painting a rosy picture of the future that goes along with the success of the project. For the "goat" the project then appears to be an opportunity, rather than a risk. I've sometimes seen scapegoats forced into the role fully aware of what was happening, and they tended to be much less tractable, although it can still work if you have just the right touch.

Why a good employee? Because chucking a poor performer at the problem is very obvious. Besides, conventional wisdom says you should put your best people on your biggest challenges. Anything less looks suspicious. The problem with this strategy is that you may very well have to sacrifice the employee, because when the project results in a failure, it is likely to be either him or you (although sometimes it can be both of you, if you stayed too close). You have to be ready to let that employee go fairly quickly, and you might even need to toss another body or two under the wheels, too.

Long-term ramifications are huge – you deplete your talent pool, and you develop a bad reputation among your subordinates by using the tactic. Oddly, I've seen it repeatedly used as standard operating procedure, or even applauded, at the highest levels of corporations – an environment typically rife with admiring maneuverers.

As the pinnacle of the political maneuverer's tactical options, scapegoating is a must for any corporate politician with an eye on the top job.

Chapter 30 – Use Sparingly, Use Strategically

The final power player tactic involves the effective selection and usage of the techniques already discussed. If you're a power player, the way you do this will differ, depending on whether you're a street fighter or a maneuverer.

Most of your coworkers – perhaps even the world at large – see the power player tactics as...well...objectionable. Or obnoxious. If you're a maneuverer, you want to avoid the label of *obnoxious*. *Obnoxious* will taint your image. *Obnoxious* will drive allies away. *Obnoxious* will add to your list of enemies and provide them with a rallying point. If you're a maneuverer, you want to prevent those things from happening, and there is no way to prevent them other than to use the tactics sparingly.

If you're of the rarer street fighter persuasion, you probably don't care much about being labeled *obnoxious*, and you will have a freer hand in using the power player tactics. In fact, people will probably expect you to be playing politics more or less all the time (which creates its own challenges because of the accumulation of enemies that naturally occurs under such circumstances).

So how do you decide when it is best to do nothing, when it is best to limit yourself to the relatively benign tactics of the neutrals, and when it is appropriate to go all out? There are four questions you must consider first:

1. Is the situation one where **high rewards** are possible? By high rewards, I mean promotion, job-preservation, or enemy elimination, rather than just image enhancement, alliance building, or revenge. If so, more aggressive tactics are in order.

2. Are the **consequences of failure** small? Every power player tactic has the potential to backfire. Every application could potentially bend back on you, if you make a mistake or encounter unexpected opposition. Are you betting a friendship with a subordinate two levels below you, or are you betting your career? High consequences of failing suggest a more cautious approach.

3. Is the **likelihood of success** high or very high? More risk can be taken, if you're almost certain it will be a win. Taking high-risk gambles, however, is a mistake, as eventually one will fall apart. I recommend you look for what seems like sure things in the beginning – as the situation unfolds and you uncover adverse circumstances, at least you still have a good chance of winning.

4. Is the **political capital cost** low? Every political project you undertake stresses your alliances and friendships. Metaphorically, you are making a withdrawal from your political capital account. You don't want to find yourself in dire need with a low balance. Save your political capital for the best opportunities.

If you can say yes to three of the four questions above, it is probably a good opportunity for a maneuverer to engage in power player tactics. If you can only say yes to one or two, my advice is to stick with neutral tactics. If you don't have any yeses, then you're just wasting your time and exposing yourself unnecessarily.

Section 5 – Final Thoughts

Chapter 31 – A Postscript

The concepts presented in this book are primarily my own work, and principally based on my own observations. The concepts were developed through my experiences with four different large employers, and interactions I've had with hundreds of employees at dozens of other large corporations.

Some of the terminology, such as *street fighters* or *maneuverers* I've adapted from the work of others, trying to stay as true as possible to their original concepts, but also wanting to adapt those descriptions to the broad landscape of my own concept.

Politics in the corporation involves two primary dimensions – will and skill.

Will comes into play in answering the question of where the practitioner draws the line between acceptable and offensive. Some eschew politics completely, while others seem to feel (either through deliberate thought, or by default) that anything goes. In some of my fictional writing, I explore the extension of that boundary to include illegal acts, as opposed to just immoral ones – things like blackmail, theft, murder, and espionage. Other than fear of punishment, what prevents an amoral executive from stopping at mere scapegoating? Why not move on to other potentially productive actions?

Skill is determined by natural talent, education, and practice. I believe that those who are the most emotionally intelligent (in other words, the most aware of how others perceive and feel about what is going on around them) have the greatest natural talent for corporate politics. Education can be academic, but in a practical sense, the aid of an astute mentor is probably the best source of political learning. And just like any human endeavor, practicing the tactics makes one better at implementing them. Alas, negative experiences probably teach more than positive ones do.

Combine both high will and skill, and you've got the makings of a successful corporate politician. But not all good politicians succeed, and not all poor politicians fail. This is because tangible, measurable job performance also counts in the corporate world – a subject I've largely ignored in this book.

Ultimately it takes all three – political skill, political will, and job performance – to keep ascending the ladder.

And there is a luck factor as well, although I've always been opposed to ascribing a large part of success and failure to luck. The belief that winners create their own luck certainly has its appeal. But I can't deny there is a certain randomness to those who ultimately ascend to the top, compared to those who don't. Some people become CEO's with obvious flaws, while others, with seemingly impenetrable armor, are terminated (although rarely with extreme prejudice). So yes, I suppose there is some luck involved in the grand scheme of things, or providence, karma or whatever else to which one attributes occurrences in this world.

I would love to hear feedback from other thinkers on the subject of politics, political tactics, and the way these things function in large organizations. Please feel free to email your questions, additions, objections, or feedback to tspears62@gmail.com.

ABOUT THE AUTHOR

Tom Spears earned a Bachelor of Science degree in Engineering from Purdue University and a Masters in Business Administration from Harvard University. He spent twenty-seven years working for four U.S. based public corporations. During fifteen of those years he held a title of President or Group President. Tom retired from his last Group President position in 2010 to pursue his interest in writing fiction. In 2011, Tom purchased a small manufacturing company in Nebraska, where he works part time. He still consults occasionally, having expertise in manufacturing, engineering, pricing, strategy, and corporate politics. Tom lives with his wife and six children in Ashland, Nebraska.

Connect with Tom Online

My website: http://www.tomspears.com/

My blog: http://outofcorporatelife.blogspot.com/

Facebook:
http://www.facebook.com/profile.php?id=1136367696

Twitter: http://twitter.com/#!/sprinklerboss62

45862971R00077

Made in the USA
Lexington, KY
14 October 2015